I0177887

PORTUGUESE
V O C A B U L A R Y

FOR ENGLISH SPEAKERS

ENGLISH
PORTUGUESE

The most useful words
To expand your lexicon and sharpen
your language skills

3000 words

Brazilian Portuguese vocabulary for English speakers - 3000 words

By Andrey Taranov

T&P Books vocabularies are intended for helping you learn, memorize and review foreign words. The dictionary is divided into themes, covering all major spheres of everyday activities, business, science, culture, etc.

The process of learning words using T&P Books' theme-based dictionaries gives you the following advantages:

- Correctly grouped source information predetermines success at subsequent stages of word memorization
- Availability of words derived from the same root allowing memorization of word units (rather than separate words)
- Small units of words facilitate the process of establishing associative links needed for consolidation of vocabulary
- Level of language knowledge can be estimated by the number of learned words

T&P Books Publishing
www.tpbooks.com

ISBN: 978-1-78767-451-6

This book is also available in E-book formats.
Please visit www.tpbooks.com or the major online bookstores.

BRAZILIAN PORTUGUESE VOCABULARY
for English speakers

T&P Books vocabularies are intended to help you learn, memorize, and review foreign words. The vocabulary contains over 3000 commonly used words arranged thematically.

- Vocabulary contains the most commonly used words
- Recommended as an addition to any language course
- Meets the needs of beginners and advanced learners of foreign languages
- Convenient for daily use, revision sessions, and self-testing activities
- Allows you to assess your vocabulary

Special features of the vocabulary

- Words are organized according to their meaning, not alphabetically
- Words are presented in three columns to facilitate the reviewing and self-testing processes
- Words in groups are divided into small blocks to facilitate the learning process
- The vocabulary offers a convenient and simple transcription of each foreign word

The vocabulary has 101 topics including:

Basic Concepts, Numbers, Colors, Months, Seasons, Units of Measurement, Clothing & Accessories, Food & Nutrition, Restaurant, Family Members, Relatives, Character, Feelings, Emotions, Diseases, City, Town, Sightseeing, Shopping, Money, House, Home, Office, Working in the Office, Import & Export, Marketing, Job Search, Sports, Education, Computer, Internet, Tools, Nature, Countries, Nationalities and more ...

TABLE OF CONTENTS

FAUNA   93

FLORA   100

COUNTRIES OF THE WORLD   104

PRONUNCIATION GUIDE

T&P phonetic alphabet	Portuguese example	English example

Vowels

[a]	baixo ['baɪʃu]	shorter than in ask
[e]	erro ['eʀu]	elm, medal
[ɛ]	leve ['lɛvə]	man, bad
[i]	lancil [lã'sil]	shorter than in feet
[o], [ɔ]	boca, orar ['bokə], [ɔ'rar]	drop, baught
[u]	urgente [ur'ʒẽtə]	book
[ã]	toranja [tu'rãʒə]	nasal [a]
[ẽ]	gente ['ʒẽtə]	fang
[ĩ]	seringa [sə'řĩgə]	nasal [i]
[õ]	ponto ['põtu]	strong
[ũ]	umbigo [ũ'bigu]	nasal [u]

Consonants

[b]	banco ['bãku]	baby, book
[d]	duche ['duʃe]	day, doctor
[dʒ]	abade [a'badʒi]	joke, general
[f]	facto ['faktu]	face, food
[g]	gorila [gu'rilə]	game, gold
[j]	feira ['fejrə]	yes, New York
[k]	claro ['klaru]	clock, kiss
[l]	Londres ['lõdrəʃ]	lace, people
[ʎ]	molho ['moʎu]	daily, million
[m]	montanha [mõ'tɐɲə]	magic, milk
[n]	novela [nu'vɛlə]	name, normal
[ɲ]	senhora [sə'ɲorə]	canyon, new
[ŋ]	marketing ['marketiŋ]	ring
[p]	prata ['pratə]	pencil, private
[s]	safira [sə'firə]	city, boss
[ʃ]	texto ['tɛʃtu]	machine, shark
[t]	teto ['tɛtu]	tourist, trip
[tʃ]	doente [do'ẽtʃi]	church, French

T&P phonetic alphabet	Portuguese example	English example
[v]	**alvo** ['alvu]	very, river
[z]	**vizinha** [vi'ziɲɐ]	zebra, please
[ʒ]	**juntos** ['ʒũtuʃ]	forge, pleasure
[w]	**sequoia** [se'kwɔjɐ]	vase, winter

ABBREVIATIONS
used in the vocabulary

English abbreviations

ab.	-	about
adj	-	adjective
adv	-	adverb
anim.	-	animate
as adj	-	attributive noun used as adjective
e.g.	-	for example
etc.	-	et cetera
fam.	-	familiar
fem.	-	feminine
form.	-	formal
inanim.	-	inanimate
masc.	-	masculine
math	-	mathematics
mil.	-	military
n	-	noun
pl	-	plural
pron.	-	pronoun
sb	-	somebody
sing.	-	singular
sth	-	something
v aux	-	auxiliary verb
vi	-	intransitive verb
vi, vt	-	intransitive, transitive verb
vt	-	transitive verb

Portuguese abbreviations

f	-	feminine noun
f pl	-	feminine plural
m	-	masculine noun
m pl	-	masculine plural
m, f	-	masculine, feminine
pl	-	plural
v aux	-	auxiliary verb

vi	-	intransitive verb
vi, vt	-	intransitive, transitive verb
vr	-	reflexive verb
vt	-	transitive verb

BASIC CONCEPTS

1. Pronouns

I, me	eu	['ew]
you	você	[vɔ'se]
he	ele	['ɛli]
she	ela	['ɛla]
we	nós	[nɔs]
you (to a group)	vocês	[vɔ'ses]
they (masc.)	eles	['ɛlis]
they (fem.)	elas	['ɛlas]

2. Greetings. Salutations

Hello! (fam.)	Oi!	[ɔj]
Hello! (form.)	Olá!	[o'la]
Good morning!	Bom dia!	[bõ 'dʒia]
Good afternoon!	Boa tarde!	['boa 'tardʒi]
Good evening!	Boa noite!	['boa 'nojtʃi]
to say hello	cumprimentar (vt)	[kũprimẽ'tar]
Hi! (hello)	Oi!	[ɔj]
greeting (n)	saudação (f)	[sawda'sãw]
to greet (vt)	saudar (vt)	[saw'dar]
How are you? (form.)	Como você está?	['kɔmu vo'se is'ta]
How are you? (fam.)	Como vai?	['kɔmu 'vaj]
What's new?	E aí, novidades?	[a a'i novi'dadʒis]
Bye-Bye! Goodbye!	Tchau!	['tʃaw]
See you soon!	Até breve!	[a'tɛ 'brɛvi]
Farewell!	Adeus!	[a'dews]
to say goodbye	despedir-se (vr)	[dʒispe'dʒirsi]
So long!	Até mais!	[a'tɛ majs]
Thank you!	Obrigado! -a!	[obri'gadu, -a]
Thank you very much!	Muito obrigado! -a!	['mwĩtu obri'gadu, -a]
You're welcome	De nada	[de 'nada]
Don't mention it!	Não tem de quê	['nãw tẽj de ke]
It was nothing	Não foi nada!	['nãw foj 'nada]
Excuse me! (fam.)	Desculpa!	[dʒis'kuwpa]
Excuse me! (form.)	Desculpe!	[dʒis'kuwpe]

to excuse (forgive)	**desculpar** (vt)	[dʒiskuw'par]
to apologize (vi)	**desculpar-se** (vr)	[dʒiskuw'parsi]
My apologies	**Me desculpe**	[mi dʒis'kuwpe]
I'm sorry!	**Desculpe!**	[dʒis'kuwpe]
to forgive (vt)	**perdoar** (vt)	[per'dwar]
It's okay! (that's all right)	**Não faz mal**	['nãw fajʒ maw]
please (adv)	**por favor**	[por fa'vor]

Don't forget!	**Não se esqueça!**	['nãw si is'kesa]
Certainly!	**Com certeza!**	[kõ ser'teza]
Of course not!	**Claro que não!**	['klaru ki 'nãw]
Okay! (I agree)	**Está bem! De acordo!**	[is'ta bẽj], [de a'kordu]
That's enough!	**Chega!**	['ʃega]

3. Questions

Who?	**Quem?**	[kẽj]
What?	**O que?**	[u ki]
Where? (at, in)	**Onde?**	['õdʒi]
Where (to)?	**Para onde?**	['para 'õdʒi]
From where?	**De onde?**	[de 'õdʒi]
When?	**Quando?**	['kwãdu]
Why? (What for?)	**Para quê?**	['para ke]
Why? (~ are you crying?)	**Por quê?**	[por 'ke]

What for?	**Para quê?**	['para ke]
How? (in what way)	**Como?**	['kɔmu]
What? (What kind of ...?)	**Qual?**	[kwaw]
Which?	**Qual?**	[kwaw]

To whom?	**A quem?**	[a kẽj]
About whom?	**De quem?**	[de kẽj]
About what?	**Do quê?**	[du ke]
With whom?	**Com quem?**	[kõ kẽj]

How many?	**Quantos? -as?**	['kwãtus, -as]
How much?	**Quanto?**	['kwãtu]
Whose?	**De quem?**	[de kẽj]

4. Prepositions

with (accompanied by)	**com**	[kõ]
without	**sem**	[sẽ]
to (indicating direction)	**a ..., para ...**	[a], ['para]
about (talking ~ ...)	**sobre ...**	['sobri]
before (in time)	**antes de ...**	['ãtʃis de]
in front of ...	**em frente de ...**	[ẽ 'frẽtʃi de]
under (beneath, below)	**debaixo de ...**	[de'baiʃu de]

above (over)	**sobre ..., em cima de ...**	['sobri], [ẽ 'sima de]
on (atop)	**em ..., sobre ...**	[ẽ], ['sobri]
from (off, out of)	**de ...**	[de]
of (made from)	**de ...**	[de]
in (e.g., ~ ten minutes)	**em ...**	[ẽ]
over (across the top of)	**por cima de ...**	[por 'sima de]

5. Function words. Adverbs. Part 1

Where? (at, in)	**Onde?**	['õdʒi]
here (adv)	**aqui**	[a'ki]
there (adv)	**lá, ali**	[la], [a'li]
somewhere (to be)	**em algum lugar**	[ẽ aw'gũ lu'gar]
nowhere (not in any place)	**em lugar nenhum**	[ẽ lu'gar ne'ɲũ]
by (near, beside)	**perto de ...**	['pɛrtu de]
by the window	**perto da janela**	['pɛrtu da ʒa'nɛla]
Where (to)?	**Para onde?**	['para 'õdʒi]
here (e.g., come ~!)	**aqui**	[a'ki]
there (e.g., to go ~)	**para lá**	['para la]
from here (adv)	**daqui**	[da'ki]
from there (adv)	**de lá, dali**	[de la], [da'li]
close (adv)	**perto**	['pɛrtu]
far (adv)	**longe**	['lõʒi]
near (e.g., ~ Paris)	**perto de ...**	['pɛrtu de]
nearby (adv)	**à mão, perto**	[a mãw], ['pɛrtu]
not far (adv)	**não fica longe**	['nãw 'fika 'lõʒi]
left (adj)	**esquerdo**	[is'kerdu]
on the left	**à esquerda**	[a is'kerda]
to the left	**para a esquerda**	['para a is'kerda]
right (adj)	**direito**	[dʒi'rejtu]
on the right	**à direita**	[a dʒi'rejta]
to the right	**para a direita**	['para a dʒi'rejta]
in front (adv)	**em frente**	[ẽ 'frẽtʃi]
front (as adj)	**da frente**	[da 'frẽtʃi]
ahead (the kids ran ~)	**adiante**	[a'dʒjãtʃi]
behind (adv)	**atrás de ...**	[a'trajs de]
from behind	**de trás**	[de trajs]
back (towards the rear)	**para trás**	['para trajs]
middle	**meio (m), metade (f)**	['meju], [me'tadʒi]
in the middle	**no meio**	[nu 'meju]

at the side	**do lado**	[du 'ladu]
everywhere (adv)	**em todo lugar**	[ẽ 'todu lu'gar]
around (in all directions)	**por todos os lados**	[por 'todus os 'ladus]
from inside	**de dentro**	[de 'dẽtru]
somewhere (to go)	**para algum lugar**	['para aw'gũ lu'gar]
straight (directly)	**diretamente**	[dʒireta'mẽtʃi]
back (e.g., come ~)	**de volta**	[de 'vɔwta]
from anywhere	**de algum lugar**	[de aw'gũ lu'gar]
from somewhere	**de algum lugar**	[de aw'gũ lu'gar]
firstly (adv)	**em primeiro lugar**	[ẽ pri'mejru lu'gar]
secondly (adv)	**em segundo lugar**	[ẽ se'gũdu lu'gar]
thirdly (adv)	**em terceiro lugar**	[ẽ ter'sejru lu'gar]
suddenly (adv)	**de repente**	[de he'pẽtʃi]
at first (in the beginning)	**no início**	[nu i'nisju]
for the first time	**pela primeira vez**	['pɛla pri'mejra 'vez]
long before ...	**muito antes de ...**	['mwĩtu 'ãtʃis de]
anew (over again)	**de novo**	[de 'novu]
for good (adv)	**para sempre**	['para 'sẽpri]
never (adv)	**nunca**	['nũka]
again (adv)	**de novo**	[de 'novu]
now (at present)	**agora**	[a'gɔra]
often (adv)	**frequentemente**	[frekwẽtʃi'mẽtʃi]
then (adv)	**então**	[ẽ'tãw]
urgently (quickly)	**urgentemente**	[urʒete'mẽtʃi]
usually (adv)	**normalmente**	[nɔrmaw'mẽtʃi]
by the way, ...	**a propósito, ...**	[a pro'pɔzitu]
possibly	**é possível**	[ɛ po'sivew]
probably (adv)	**provavelmente**	[provavɛw'mẽtʃi]
maybe (adv)	**talvez**	[taw'vez]
besides ...	**além disso, ...**	[a'lẽj 'dʒisu]
that's why ...	**por isso ...**	[por 'isu]
in spite of ...	**apesar de ...**	[ape'zar de]
thanks to ...	**graças a ...**	['grasas a]
what (pron.)	**que**	[ki]
that (conj.)	**que**	[ki]
something	**algo**	[awgu]
anything (something)	**alguma coisa**	[aw'guma 'kojza]
nothing	**nada**	['nada]
who (pron.)	**quem**	[kẽj]
someone	**alguém**	[aw'gẽj]
somebody	**alguém**	[aw'gẽj]
nobody	**ninguém**	[nĩ'gẽj]
nowhere (a voyage to ~)	**para lugar nenhum**	['para lu'gar ne'ɲũ]

| nobody's | de ninguém | [de nĩ'gẽj] |
| somebody's | de alguém | [de aw'gẽj] |

so (I'm ~ glad)	tão	[tãw]
also (as well)	também	[tã'bẽj]
too (as well)	também	[tã'bẽj]

6. Function words. Adverbs. Part 2

Why?	Por quê?	[por 'ke]
for some reason	por alguma razão	[por aw'guma ha'zãw]
because ...	porque ...	[por'ke]
for some purpose	por qualquer razão	[por kwaw'ker ha'zãw]

and	e	[i]
or	ou	['o]
but	mas	[mas]
for (e.g., ~ me)	para	['para]

too (~ many people)	muito, demais	['mwĩtu], [dʒi'majs]
only (exclusively)	só, somente	[sɔ], [sɔ'mẽtʃi]
exactly (adv)	exatamente	[ɛzata'mẽtʃi]
about (more or less)	cerca de ...	['serka de]

approximately (adv)	aproximadamente	[aprosimada'mẽti]
approximate (adj)	aproximado	[aprosi'madu]
almost (adv)	quase	['kwazi]
the rest	resto (m)	['hɛstu]

the other (second)	o outro	[u 'otru]
other (different)	outro	['otru]
each (adj)	cada	['kada]
any (no matter which)	qualquer	[kwaw'ker]
many (adj)	muitos, muitas	['mwĩtos], ['mwĩtas]
much (adv)	muito	['mwĩtu]
many people	muitas pessoas	['mwĩtas pe'soas]
all (everyone)	todos	['todus]

in return for ...	em troca de ...	[ẽ 'trɔka de]
in exchange (adv)	em troca	[ẽ 'trɔka]
by hand (made)	à mão	[a mãw]
hardly (negative opinion)	pouco provável	['poku pro'vavew]

probably (adv)	provavelmente	[provavɛw'mẽtʃi]
on purpose (intentionally)	de propósito	[de pro'pɔzitu]
by accident (adv)	por acidente	[por asi'dẽtʃi]

very (adv)	muito	['mwĩtu]
for example (adv)	por exemplo	[por e'zẽplu]
between	entre	['ẽtri]

among	**entre, no meio de ...**	['ẽtri], [nu 'meju de]
so much (such a lot)	**tanto**	['tãtu]
especially (adv)	**especialmente**	[ispesjal'mẽte]

NUMBERS. MISCELLANEOUS

7. Cardinal numbers. Part 1

0 zero	zero	['zɛru]
1 one	um	[ũ]
2 two	dois	['dojs]
3 three	três	[tres]
4 four	quatro	['kwatru]
5 five	cinco	['sĩku]
6 six	seis	[sejs]
7 seven	sete	['sɛtʃi]
8 eight	oito	['ojtu]
9 nine	nove	['nɔvi]
10 ten	dez	[dɛz]
11 eleven	onze	['õzi]
12 twelve	doze	['dozi]
13 thirteen	treze	['trezi]
14 fourteen	catorze	[ka'torzi]
15 fifteen	quinze	['kĩzi]
16 sixteen	dezesseis	[deze'sejs]
17 seventeen	dezessete	[dezi'setʃi]
18 eighteen	dezoito	[dʒi'zojtu]
19 nineteen	dezenove	[deze'nɔvi]
20 twenty	vinte	['vĩtʃi]
21 twenty-one	vinte e um	['vĩtʃi i ũ]
22 twenty-two	vinte e dois	['vĩtʃi i 'dojs]
23 twenty-three	vinte e três	['vĩtʃi i 'tres]
30 thirty	trinta	['trĩta]
31 thirty-one	trinta e um	['trĩta i ũ]
32 thirty-two	trinta e dois	['trĩta i 'dojs]
33 thirty-three	trinta e três	['trĩta i 'tres]
40 forty	quarenta	[kwa'rẽta]
41 forty-one	quarenta e um	[kwa'rẽta i 'ũ]
42 forty-two	quarenta e dois	[kwa'rẽta i 'dojs]
43 forty-three	quarenta e três	[kwa'rẽta i 'tres]
50 fifty	cinquenta	[sĩ'kwẽta]
51 fifty-one	cinquenta e um	[sĩ'kwẽta i ũ]
52 fifty-two	cinquenta e dois	[sĩ'kwẽta i 'dojs]

53 fifty-three	cinquenta e três	[sĩ'kwẽta i 'tres]
60 sixty	sessenta	[se'sẽta]
61 sixty-one	sessenta e um	[se'sẽta i ũ]
62 sixty-two	sessenta e dois	[se'sẽta i 'dojs]
63 sixty-three	sessenta e três	[se'sẽta i 'tres]

70 seventy	setenta	[se'tẽta]
71 seventy-one	setenta e um	[se'tẽta i ũ]
72 seventy-two	setenta e dois	[se'tẽta i 'dojs]
73 seventy-three	setenta e três	[se'tẽta i 'tres]

80 eighty	oitenta	[oj'tẽta]
81 eighty-one	oitenta e um	[oj'tẽta i 'ũ]
82 eighty-two	oitenta e dois	[oj'tẽta i 'dojs]
83 eighty-three	oitenta e três	[oj'tẽta i 'tres]

90 ninety	noventa	[no'vẽta]
91 ninety-one	noventa e um	[no'vẽta i 'ũ]
92 ninety-two	noventa e dois	[no'vẽta i 'dojs]
93 ninety-three	noventa e três	[no'vẽta i 'tres]

8. Cardinal numbers. Part 2

100 one hundred	cem	[sẽ]
200 two hundred	duzentos	[du'zẽtus]
300 three hundred	trezentos	[tre'zẽtus]
400 four hundred	quatrocentos	[kwatro'sẽtus]
500 five hundred	quinhentos	[ki'ɲẽtus]

600 six hundred	seiscentos	[sej'sẽtus]
700 seven hundred	setecentos	[sete'sẽtus]
800 eight hundred	oitocentos	[ojtu'sẽtus]
900 nine hundred	novecentos	[nove'sẽtus]

1000 one thousand	mil	[miw]
2000 two thousand	dois mil	['dojs miw]
3000 three thousand	três mil	['tres miw]
10000 ten thousand	dez mil	['dɛz miw]
one hundred thousand	cem mil	[sẽ miw]
million	um milhão	[ũ mi'ʎãw]
billion	um bilhão	[ũ bi'ʎãw]

9. Ordinal numbers

first (adj)	primeiro	[pri'mejru]
second (adj)	segundo	[se'gũdu]
third (adj)	terceiro	[ter'sejru]
fourth (adj)	quarto	['kwartu]

fifth (adj)	quinto	['kĩtu]
sixth (adj)	sexto	['sestu]
seventh (adj)	sétimo	['sɛtʃimu]
eighth (adj)	oitavo	[oj'tavu]
ninth (adj)	nono	['nonu]
tenth (adj)	décimo	['dɛsimu]

COLOURS. UNITS OF MEASUREMENT

10. Colors

color	cor (f)	[kɔr]
shade (tint)	tom (m)	[tõ]
hue	tonalidade (m)	[tonali'dadʒi]
rainbow	arco-íris (m)	['arku 'iris]
white (adj)	branco	['brãku]
black (adj)	preto	['pretu]
gray (adj)	cinza	['sĩza]
green (adj)	verde	['verdʒi]
yellow (adj)	amarelo	[ama'rɛlu]
red (adj)	vermelho	[ver'meʎu]
blue (adj)	azul	[a'zuw]
light blue (adj)	azul claro	[a'zuw 'klaru]
pink (adj)	rosa	['hɔza]
orange (adj)	laranja	[la'rãʒa]
violet (adj)	violeta	[vjo'leta]
brown (adj)	marrom	[ma'hõ]
golden (adj)	dourado	[do'radu]
silvery (adj)	prateado	[pra'tʃadu]
beige (adj)	bege	['bɛʒi]
cream (adj)	creme	['krɛmi]
turquoise (adj)	turquesa	[tur'keza]
cherry red (adj)	vermelho cereja	[ver'meʎu se'reʒa]
lilac (adj)	lilás	[li'las]
crimson (adj)	carmim	[kah'mĩ]
light (adj)	claro	['klaru]
dark (adj)	escuro	[is'kuru]
bright, vivid (adj)	vivo	['vivu]
colored (pencils)	de cor	[de kɔr]
color (e.g., ~ film)	a cores	[a 'kores]
black-and-white (adj)	preto e branco	['pretu i 'brãku]
plain (one-colored)	de uma só cor	[de 'uma sɔ kɔr]
multicolored (adj)	multicolor	[muwtʃiko'lor]

11. Units of measurement

weight	**peso** (m)	['pezu]
length	**comprimento** (m)	[kõpri'mẽtu]
width	**largura** (f)	[lar'gura]
height	**altura** (f)	[aw'tura]
depth	**profundidade** (f)	[profũdʒi'dadʒi]
volume	**volume** (m)	[vo'lumi]
area	**área** (f)	['arja]

gram	**grama** (m)	['grama]
milligram	**miligrama** (m)	[mili'grama]
kilogram	**quilograma** (m)	[kilo'grama]
ton	**tonelada** (f)	[tune'lada]
pound	**libra** (f)	['libra]
ounce	**onça** (f)	['õsa]

meter	**metro** (m)	['mɛtru]
millimeter	**milímetro** (m)	[mi'limetru]
centimeter	**centímetro** (m)	[sẽ'tʃimetru]
kilometer	**quilômetro** (m)	[ki'lometru]
mile	**milha** (f)	['miʎa]

inch	**polegada** (f)	[pole'gada]
foot	**pé** (m)	[pɛ]
yard	**jarda** (f)	['ʒarda]

square meter	**metro** (m) **quadrado**	['mɛtru kwa'dradu]
hectare	**hectare** (m)	[ek'tari]

liter	**litro** (m)	['litru]
degree	**grau** (m)	[graw]
volt	**volt** (m)	['vɔwtʃi]
ampere	**ampère** (m)	[ã'pɛri]
horsepower	**cavalo** (m) **de potência**	[ka'valu de po'tẽsja]

quantity	**quantidade** (f)	[kwãtʃi'dadʒi]
a little bit of ...	**um pouco de ...**	[ũ 'poku de]
half	**metade** (f)	[me'tadʒi]

dozen	**dúzia** (f)	['duzja]
piece (item)	**peça** (f)	['pɛsa]

size	**tamanho** (m), **dimensão** (f)	[ta'maɲu], [dʒimẽ'sãw]
scale (map ~)	**escala** (f)	[is'kala]

minimal (adj)	**mínimo**	['minimu]
the smallest (adj)	**menor, mais pequeno**	[me'nɔr], [majs pe'kenu]
medium (adj)	**médio**	['mɛdʒju]
maximal (adj)	**máximo**	['masimu]
the largest (adj)	**maior, mais grande**	[ma'jɔr], [majs 'grãdʒi]

12. Containers

canning jar (glass ~)	pote (m) de vidro	['potʃi de 'vidru]
can	lata (f)	['lata]
bucket	balde (m)	['bawdʒi]
barrel	barril (m)	[ba'hiw]

wash basin (e.g., plastic ~)	bacia (f)	[ba'sia]
tank (100L water ~)	tanque (m)	['tãki]
hip flask	cantil (m) de bolso	[kã'tʃiw dʒi 'bowsu]
jerrycan	galão (m) de gasolina	[ga'lãw de gazo'lina]
tank (e.g., tank car)	cisterna (f)	[sis'tɛrna]

mug	caneca (f)	[ka'nɛka]
cup (of coffee, etc.)	xícara (f)	['ʃikara]
saucer	pires (m)	['piris]
glass (tumbler)	copo (m)	['kɔpu]
wine glass	taça (f) de vinho	['tasa de 'viɲu]
stock pot (soup pot)	panela (f)	[pa'nɛla]

| bottle (~ of wine) | garrafa (f) | [ga'hafa] |
| neck (of the bottle, etc.) | gargalo (m) | [gar'galu] |

carafe (decanter)	jarra (f)	['ʒaha]
pitcher	jarro (m)	['ʒahu]
vessel (container)	recipiente (m)	[hesi'pjẽtʃi]
pot (crock, stoneware ~)	pote (m)	['potʃi]
vase	vaso (m)	['vazu]

flacon, bottle (perfume ~)	frasco (m)	['frasku]
vial, small bottle	frasquinho (m)	[fras'kiɲu]
tube (of toothpaste)	tubo (m)	['tubu]

sack (bag)	saco (m)	['saku]
bag (paper ~, plastic ~)	sacola (f)	[sa'kɔla]
pack (of cigarettes, etc.)	maço (m)	['masu]

box (e.g., shoebox)	caixa (f)	['kaɪʃa]
crate	caixote (m)	[kaj'ʃɔtʃi]
basket	cesto (m)	['sestu]

MAIN VERBS

13. The most important verbs. Part 1

to advise (vt)	**aconselhar** (vt)	[akõse'ʎar]
to agree (say yes)	**concordar** (vi)	[kõkor'dar]
to answer (vi, vt)	**responder** (vt)	[hespõ'der]
to apologize (vi)	**desculpar-se** (vr)	[dʒiskuw'parsi]
to arrive (vi)	**chegar** (vi)	[ʃe'gar]
to ask (~ oneself)	**perguntar** (vt)	[pergũ'tar]
to ask (~ sb to do sth)	**pedir** (vt)	[pe'dʒir]
to be (~ a teacher)	**ser** (vi)	[ser]
to be (~ on a diet)	**estar** (vi)	[is'tar]
to be afraid	**ter medo**	[ter 'medu]
to be hungry	**ter fome**	[ter 'fɔmi]
to be interested in ...	**interessar-se** (vr)	[ĩtere'sarsi]
to be needed	**ser necessário**	[ser nese'sarju]
to be surprised	**surpreender-se** (vr)	[surprjẽ'dersi]
to be thirsty	**ter sede**	[ter 'sedʒi]
to begin (vt)	**começar** (vt)	[kome'sar]
to belong to ...	**pertencer** (vt)	[pertẽ'ser]
to boast (vi)	**gabar-se** (vr)	[ga'barsi]
to break (split into pieces)	**quebrar** (vt)	[ke'brar]
to call (~ for help)	**chamar** (vt)	[ʃa'mar]
can (v aux)	**poder** (vi)	[po'der]
to catch (vt)	**pegar** (vt)	[pe'gar]
to change (vt)	**mudar** (vt)	[mu'dar]
to choose (select)	**escolher** (vt)	[isko'ʎer]
to come down (the stairs)	**descer** (vi)	[de'ser]
to compare (vt)	**comparar** (vt)	[kõpa'rar]
to complain (vi, vt)	**queixar-se** (vr)	[kej'ʃarsi]
to confuse (mix up)	**confundir** (vt)	[kõfũ'dʒir]
to continue (vt)	**continuar** (vt)	[kõtʃi'nwar]
to control (vt)	**controlar** (vt)	[kõtro'lar]
to cook (dinner)	**preparar** (vt)	[prepa'rar]
to cost (vt)	**custar** (vt)	[kus'tar]
to count (add up)	**contar** (vt)	[kõ'tar]
to count on ...	**contar com ...**	[kõ'tar kõ]
to create (vt)	**criar** (vt)	[krjar]
to cry (weep)	**chorar** (vi)	[ʃo'rar]

14. The most important verbs. Part 2

to deceive (vi, vt)	enganar (vt)	[ẽga'nar]
to decorate (tree, street)	decorar (vt)	[deko'rar]
to defend (a country, etc.)	defender (vt)	[defẽ'der]
to demand (request firmly)	exigir (vt)	[ezi'ʒir]
to dig (vt)	cavar (vt)	[ka'var]
to discuss (vt)	discutir (vt)	[dʒisku'tʃir]
to do (vt)	fazer (vt)	[fa'zer]
to doubt (have doubts)	duvidar (vt)	[duvi'dar]
to drop (let fall)	deixar cair (vt)	[dej'ʃar ka'ir]
to enter	entrar (vi)	[ẽ'trar]
(room, house, etc.)		
to excuse (forgive)	desculpar (vt)	[dʒiskuw'par]
to exist (vi)	existir (vi)	[ezis'tʃir]
to expect (foresee)	prever (vt)	[pre'ver]
to explain (vt)	explicar (vt)	[ispli'kar]
to fall (vi)	cair (vi)	[ka'ir]
to find (vt)	encontrar (vt)	[ẽkõ'trar]
to finish (vt)	acabar, terminar (vt)	[aka'bar], [termi'nar]
to fly (vi)	voar (vi)	[vo'ar]
to follow ... (come after)	seguir ...	[se'gir]
to forget (vi, vt)	esquecer (vt)	[iske'ser]
to forgive (vt)	perdoar (vt)	[per'dwar]
to give (vt)	dar (vt)	[dar]
to give a hint	dar uma dica	[dar 'uma 'dʒika]
to go (on foot)	ir (vi)	[ir]
to go for a swim	ir nadar	[ir na'dar]
to go out (for dinner, etc.)	sair (vi)	[sa'ir]
to guess (the answer)	adivinhar (vt)	[adʒivi'ɲar]
to have (vt)	ter (vt)	[ter]
to have breakfast	tomar café da manhã	[to'mar ka'fɛ da ma'ɲã]
to have dinner	jantar (vi)	[ʒã'tar]
to have lunch	almoçar (vi)	[awmo'sar]
to hear (vt)	ouvir (vt)	[o'vir]
to help (vt)	ajudar (vt)	[aʒu'dar]
to hide (vt)	esconder (vt)	[iskõ'der]
to hope (vi, vt)	esperar (vi, vt)	[ispe'rar]
to hunt (vi, vt)	caçar (vi)	[ka'sar]
to hurry (vi)	apressar-se (vr)	[apre'sarsi]

15. The most important verbs. Part 3

to inform (vt)	informar (vt)	[ĩfor'mar]
to insist (vi, vt)	insistir (vi)	[ĩsis'tʃir]
to insult (vt)	insultar (vt)	[ĩsuw'tar]
to invite (vt)	convidar (vt)	[kõvi'dar]
to joke (vi)	brincar (vi)	[brĩ'kar]
to keep (vt)	guardar (vt)	[gwar'dar]
to keep silent, to hush	ficar em silêncio	[fi'kar ẽ si'lẽsju]
to kill (vt)	matar (vt)	[ma'tar]
to know (sb)	conhecer (vt)	[koɲe'ser]
to know (sth)	saber (vt)	[sa'ber]
to laugh (vi)	rir (vi)	[hir]
to liberate (city, etc.)	libertar, liberar (vt)	[liber'tar], [libe'rar]
to like (I like …)	gostar (vt)	[gos'tar]
to look for … (search)	buscar (vt)	[bus'kar]
to love (sb)	amar (vt)	[a'mar]
to make a mistake	errar (vi)	[e'har]
to manage, to run	dirigir (vt)	[dʒiri'ʒir]
to mean (signify)	significar (vt)	[signifi'kar]
to mention (talk about)	mencionar (vt)	[mẽsjo'nar]
to miss (school, etc.)	faltar a …	[faw'tar a]
to notice (see)	perceber (vt)	[perse'ber]
to object (vi, vt)	objetar (vt)	[obʒe'tar]
to observe (see)	observar (vt)	[obser'var]
to open (vt)	abrir (vt)	[a'brir]
to order (meal, etc.)	pedir (vt)	[pe'dʒir]
to order (mil.)	ordenar (vt)	[orde'nar]
to own (possess)	possuir (vt)	[po'swir]
to participate (vi)	participar (vi)	[partʃisi'par]
to pay (vi, vt)	pagar (vt)	[pa'gar]
to permit (vt)	permitir (vt)	[permi'tʃir]
to plan (vt)	planejar (vt)	[plane'ʒar]
to play (children)	brincar, jogar (vi, vt)	[brĩ'kar], [ʒo'gar]
to pray (vi, vt)	rezar, orar (vi)	[he'zar], [o'rar]
to prefer (vt)	preferir (vt)	[prefe'rir]
to promise (vt)	prometer (vt)	[prome'ter]
to pronounce (vt)	pronunciar (vt)	[pronũ'sjar]
to propose (vt)	propor (vt)	[pro'por]
to punish (vt)	punir (vt)	[pu'nir]

16. The most important verbs. Part 4

to read (vi, vt)	ler (vt)	[ler]
to recommend (vt)	recomendar (vt)	[hekomẽ'dar]

to refuse (vi, vt)	**negar-se** (vt)	[ne'garsi]
to regret (be sorry)	**arrepender-se** (vr)	[ahepẽ'dersi]
to rent (sth from sb)	**alugar** (vt)	[alu'gar]
to repeat (say again)	**repetir** (vt)	[hepe'tʃir]
to reserve, to book	**reservar** (vt)	[hezer'var]
to run (vi)	**correr** (vi)	[ko'her]
to save (rescue)	**salvar** (vt)	[saw'var]
to say (~ thank you)	**dizer** (vt)	[dʒi'zer]
to scold (vt)	**ralhar, repreender** (vt)	[ha'ʎar], [heprjẽ'der]
to see (vt)	**ver** (vt)	[ver]
to sell (vt)	**vender** (vt)	[vẽ'der]
to send (vt)	**enviar** (vt)	[ẽ'vjar]
to shoot (vi)	**disparar, atirar** (vi)	[dʒispa'rar], [atʃi'rar]
to shout (vi)	**gritar** (vi)	[gri'tar]
to show (vt)	**mostrar** (vt)	[mos'trar]
to sign (document)	**assinar** (vt)	[asi'nar]
to sit down (vi)	**sentar-se** (vr)	[sẽ'tarsi]
to smile (vi)	**sorrir** (vi)	[so'hir]
to speak (vi, vt)	**falar** (vi)	[fa'lar]
to steal (money, etc.)	**roubar** (vt)	[ho'bar]
to stop (for pause, etc.)	**parar** (vi)	[pa'rar]
to stop (please ~ calling me)	**cessar** (vt)	[se'sar]
to study (vt)	**estudar** (vt)	[istu'dar]
to swim (vi)	**nadar** (vi)	[na'dar]
to take (vt)	**pegar** (vt)	[pe'gar]
to think (vi, vt)	**pensar** (vi, vt)	[pẽ'sar]
to threaten (vt)	**ameaçar** (vt)	[amea'sar]
to touch (with hands)	**tocar** (vt)	[to'kar]
to translate (vt)	**traduzir** (vt)	[tradu'zir]
to trust (vt)	**confiar** (vt)	[kõ'fjar]
to try (attempt)	**tentar** (vt)	[tẽ'tar]
to turn (e.g., ~ left)	**virar** (vi)	[vi'rar]
to underestimate (vt)	**subestimar** (vt)	[subestʃi'mar]
to understand (vt)	**entender** (vt)	[ẽtẽ'der]
to unite (vt)	**unir** (vt)	[u'nir]
to wait (vt)	**esperar** (vt)	[ispe'rar]
to want (wish, desire)	**querer** (vt)	[ke'rer]
to warn (vt)	**advertir** (vt)	[adʒiver'tʃir]
to work (vi)	**trabalhar** (vi)	[traba'ʎar]
to write (vt)	**escrever** (vt)	[iskre'ver]
to write down	**anotar** (vt)	[ano'tar]

TIME. CALENDAR

17. Weekdays

Monday	segunda-feira (f)	[se'gŭda-'fejra]
Tuesday	terça-feira (f)	['tersa 'fejra]
Wednesday	quarta-feira (f)	['kwarta-'fejra]
Thursday	quinta-feira (f)	['kĭta-'fejra]
Friday	sexta-feira (f)	['sesta-'fejra]
Saturday	sábado (m)	['sabadu]
Sunday	domingo (m)	[do'mĭgu]
today (adv)	hoje	['oʒi]
tomorrow (adv)	amanhã	[ama'ɲã]
the day after tomorrow	depois de amanhã	[de'pojs de ama'ɲã]
yesterday (adv)	ontem	['ŏtẽ]
the day before yesterday	anteontem	[ãtʃi'ŏtẽ]
day	dia (m)	['dʒia]
working day	dia (m) de trabalho	['dʒia de tra'baʎu]
public holiday	feriado (m)	[fe'rjadu]
day off	dia (m) de folga	['dʒia de 'fowga]
weekend	fim (m) de semana	[fĩ de se'mana]
all day long	o dia todo	[u 'dʒia 'todu]
the next day (adv)	no dia seguinte	[nu 'dʒia se'gĭtʃi]
two days ago	há dois dias	[a 'dojs 'dʒias]
the day before	na véspera	[na 'vɛspera]
daily (adj)	diário	['dʒjarju]
every day (adv)	todos os dias	['todus us 'dʒias]
week	semana (f)	[se'mana]
last week (adv)	na semana passada	[na se'mana pa'sada]
next week (adv)	semana que vem	[se'mana ke vẽj]
weekly (adj)	semanal	[sema'naw]
every week (adv)	toda semana	['tɔda se'mana]
twice a week	duas vezes por semana	['duas 'vezis por se'mana]
every Tuesday	toda terça-feira	['tɔda tersa 'fejra]

18. Hours. Day and night

morning	manhã (f)	[ma'ɲã]
in the morning	de manhã	[de ma'ɲã]
noon, midday	meio-dia (m)	['meju 'dʒia]

in the afternoon	à tarde	[a 'tardʒi]
evening	tardinha (f)	[tar'dʒiɲa]
in the evening	à tardinha	[a tar'dʒiɲa]
night	noite (f)	['nojtʃi]
at night	à noite	[a 'nojtʃi]
midnight	meia-noite (f)	['meja 'nojtʃi]

second	segundo (m)	[se'gũdu]
minute	minuto (m)	[mi'nutu]
hour	hora (f)	['ɔra]
half an hour	meia hora (f)	['meja 'ɔra]
a quarter-hour	quarto (m) de hora	['kwartu de 'ɔra]
fifteen minutes	quinze minutos	['kĩzi mi'nutus]
24 hours	vinte e quatro horas	['vĩtʃi i 'kwatru 'ɔras]

sunrise	nascer (m) do sol	[na'ser du sɔw]
dawn	amanhecer (m)	[amaɲe'ser]
early morning	madrugada (f)	[madru'gada]
sunset	pôr-do-sol (m)	[por du 'sɔw]

early in the morning	de madrugada	[de madru'gada]
this morning	esta manhã	['ɛsta ma'ɲã]
tomorrow morning	amanhã de manhã	[ama'ɲã de ma'ɲã]

this afternoon	esta tarde	['ɛsta 'tardʒi]
in the afternoon	à tarde	[a 'tardʒi]
tomorrow afternoon	amanhã à tarde	[ama'ɲã a 'tardʒi]

| tonight (this evening) | esta noite, hoje à noite | ['ɛsta 'nojtʃi], ['oʒi a 'nojtʃi] |
| tomorrow night | amanhã à noite | [ama'ɲã a 'nojtʃi] |

at 3 o'clock sharp	às três horas em ponto	[as tres 'ɔras ẽ 'põtu]
about 4 o'clock	por volta das quatro	[por 'vɔwta das 'kwatru]
by 12 o'clock	às doze	[as 'dozi]

in 20 minutes	em vinte minutos	[ẽ 'vĩtʃi mi'nutus]
in an hour	em uma hora	[ẽ 'uma 'ɔra]
on time (adv)	a tempo	[a 'tẽpu]

a quarter to …	… um quarto para	[… ũ 'kwartu 'para]
within an hour	dentro de uma hora	['dẽtru de 'uma 'ɔra]
every 15 minutes	a cada quinze minutos	[a 'kada 'kĩzi mi'nutus]
round the clock	as vinte e quatro horas	[as 'vĩtʃi i 'kwatru 'ɔras]

19. Months. Seasons

January	janeiro (m)	[ʒa'nejru]
February	fevereiro (m)	[feve'rejru]
March	março (m)	['marsu]
April	abril (m)	[a'briw]

| May | **maio** (m) | ['maju] |
| June | **junho** (m) | ['ʒuɲu] |

July	**julho** (m)	['ʒuʎu]
August	**agosto** (m)	[a'gostu]
September	**setembro** (m)	[se'tẽbru]
October	**outubro** (m)	[o'tubru]
November	**novembro** (m)	[no'vẽbru]
December	**dezembro** (m)	[de'zẽbru]

spring	**primavera** (f)	[prima'vɛra]
in spring	**na primavera**	[na prima'vɛra]
spring (as adj)	**primaveril**	[primave'riw]

summer	**verão** (m)	[ve'rãw]
in summer	**no verão**	[nu ve'rãw]
summer (as adj)	**de verão**	[de ve'rãw]

fall	**outono** (m)	[o'tɔnu]
in fall	**no outono**	[nu o'tɔnu]
fall (as adj)	**outonal**	[oto'naw]

winter	**inverno** (m)	[ĩ'vɛrnu]
in winter	**no inverno**	[nu ĩ'vɛrnu]
winter (as adj)	**de inverno**	[de ĩ'vɛrnu]

month	**mês** (m)	[mes]
this month	**este mês**	['estʃi mes]
next month	**mês que vem**	['mes ki vẽj]
last month	**no mês passado**	[no mes pa'sadu]

a month ago	**um mês atrás**	[ũ 'mes a'trajs]
in a month (a month later)	**em um mês**	[ẽ ũ mes]
in 2 months (2 months later)	**em dois meses**	[ẽ dojs 'mezis]
the whole month	**todo o mês**	['todu u mes]
all month long	**um mês inteiro**	[ũ mes ĩ'tejru]

monthly (~ magazine)	**mensal**	[mẽ'saw]
monthly (adv)	**mensalmente**	[mẽsaw'mẽtʃi]
every month	**todo mês**	['todu 'mes]
twice a month	**duas vezes por mês**	['duas 'vezis por mes]

year	**ano** (m)	['anu]
this year	**este ano**	['estʃi 'anu]
next year	**ano que vem**	['anu ki vẽj]
last year	**no ano passado**	[nu 'anu pa'sadu]

a year ago	**há um ano**	[a ũ 'anu]
in a year	**em um ano**	[ẽ ũ 'anu]
in two years	**dentro de dois anos**	['dẽtru de 'dojs 'anus]
the whole year	**todo o ano**	['todu u 'anu]

all year long	um ano inteiro	[ũ 'anu ĩ'tejru]
every year	cada ano	['kada 'anu]
annual (adj)	anual	[a'nwaw]
annually (adv)	anualmente	[anwaw'mẽte]
4 times a year	quatro vezes por ano	['kwatru 'vezis por 'anu]

date (e.g., today's ~)	data (f)	['data]
date (e.g., ~ of birth)	data (f)	['data]
calendar	calendário (m)	[kalẽ'darju]

half a year	meio ano	['meju 'anu]
six months	seis meses	[sejs 'mezis]
season (summer, etc.)	estação (f)	[ista'sãw]
century	século (m)	['sɛkulu]

TRAVEL. HOTEL

20. Trip. Travel

tourism, travel	**turismo** (m)	[tu'rizmu]
tourist	**turista** (m)	[tu'rista]
trip, voyage	**viagem** (f)	['vjaʒẽ]
adventure	**aventura** (f)	[avẽ'tura]
trip, journey	**viagem** (f)	['vjaʒẽ]
vacation	**férias** (f pl)	['fɛrjas]
to be on vacation	**estar de férias**	[is'tar de 'fɛrjas]
rest	**descanso** (m)	[dʒis'kãsu]
train	**trem** (m)	[trẽj]
by train	**de trem**	[de trẽj]
airplane	**avião** (m)	[a'vjãw]
by airplane	**de avião**	[de a'vjãw]
by car	**de carro**	[de 'kaho]
by ship	**de navio**	[de na'viu]
luggage	**bagagem** (f)	[ba'gaʒẽ]
suitcase	**mala** (f)	['mala]
luggage cart	**carrinho** (m)	[ka'hiɲu]
passport	**passaporte** (m)	[pasa'pɔrtʃi]
visa	**visto** (m)	['vistu]
ticket	**passagem** (f)	[pa'saʒẽ]
air ticket	**passagem** (f) **aérea**	[pa'saʒẽ a'erja]
guidebook	**guia** (m) **de viagem**	['gia de vi'aʒẽ]
map (tourist ~)	**mapa** (m)	['mapa]
area (rural ~)	**área** (f)	['arja]
place, site	**lugar** (m)	[lu'gar]
exotica (n)	**exotismo** (m)	[ezo'tʃizmu]
exotic (adj)	**exótico**	[e'zɔtʃiku]
amazing (adj)	**surpreendente**	[surprjẽ'dẽtʃi]
group	**grupo** (m)	['grupu]
excursion, sightseeing tour	**excursão** (f)	[iskur'sãw]
guide (person)	**guia** (m)	['gia]

21. Hotel

hotel	**hotel** (m)	[o'tɛw]
motel	**motel** (m)	[mo'tɛw]
three-star (~ hotel)	**três estrelas**	['tres is'trelas]
five-star	**cinco estrelas**	['sĩku is'trelas]
to stay (in a hotel, etc.)	**ficar** (vi, vt)	[fi'kar]
room	**quarto** (m)	['kwartu]
single room	**quarto** (m) **individual**	['kwartu ĩdʒivi'dwaw]
double room	**quarto** (m) **duplo**	['kwartu 'duplu]
to book a room	**reservar um quarto**	[hezer'var ũ 'kwartu]
half board	**meia pensão** (f)	['meja pẽ'sãw]
full board	**pensão** (f) **completa**	[pẽ'sãw kõ'plɛta]
with bath	**com banheira**	[kõ ba'ɲejra]
with shower	**com chuveiro**	[kõ ʃu'vejru]
satellite television	**televisão** (m) **por satélite**	[televi'zãw por sa'tɛlitʃi]
air-conditioner	**ar** (m) **condicionado**	[ar kõdʒisjo'nadu]
towel	**toalha** (f)	[to'aʎa]
key	**chave** (f)	['ʃavi]
administrator	**administrador** (m)	[adʒiministra'dor]
chambermaid	**camareira** (f)	[kama'rejra]
porter, bellboy	**bagageiro** (m)	[baga'ʒejru]
doorman	**porteiro** (m)	[por'tejru]
restaurant	**restaurante** (m)	[hestaw'rãtʃi]
pub, bar	**bar** (m)	[bar]
breakfast	**café** (m) **da manhã**	[ka'fɛ da ma'ɲã]
dinner	**jantar** (m)	[ʒã'tar]
buffet	**bufê** (m)	[bu'fe]
lobby	**saguão** (m)	[sa'gwãw]
elevator	**elevador** (m)	[eleva'dor]
DO NOT DISTURB	**NÃO PERTURBE**	['nãw per'turbi]
NO SMOKING	**PROIBIDO FUMAR!**	[proi'bidu fu'mar]

22. Sightseeing

monument	**monumento** (m)	[monu'mẽtu]
fortress	**fortaleza** (f)	[forta'leza]
palace	**palácio** (m)	[pa'lasju]
castle	**castelo** (m)	[kas'tɛlu]
tower	**torre** (f)	['tohi]
mausoleum	**mausoléu** (m)	[mawzo'lɛw]

architecture	arquitetura (f)	[arkite'tura]
medieval (adj)	medieval	[medʒje'vaw]
ancient (adj)	antigo	[ã'tʃigu]
national (adj)	nacional	[nasjo'naw]
famous (monument, etc.)	famoso	[fa'mozu]

tourist	turista (m)	[tu'rista]
guide (person)	guia (m)	['gia]
excursion, sightseeing tour	excursão (f)	[iskur'sãw]
to show (vt)	mostrar (vt)	[mos'trar]
to tell (vt)	contar (vt)	[kõ'tar]

to find (vt)	encontrar (vt)	[ẽkõ'trar]
to get lost (lose one's way)	perder-se (vr)	[per'dersi]
map (e.g., subway ~)	mapa (m)	['mapa]
map (e.g., city ~)	mapa (m)	['mapa]

souvenir, gift	lembrança (f), presente (m)	[lẽ'brãsa], [pre'zẽtʃi]
gift shop	loja (f) de presentes	['lɔʒa de pre'zẽtʃis]
to take pictures	tirar fotos	[tʃi'rar 'fotus]
to have one's picture taken	fotografar-se (vr)	[fotogra'farse]

TRANSPORTATION

23. Airport

airport	**aeroporto** (m)	[aero'portu]
airplane	**avião** (m)	[a'vjãw]
airline	**companhia** (f) **aérea**	[kõpa'ɲia a'erja]
air traffic controller	**controlador** (m) **de tráfego aéreo**	[kõtrola'dor de 'trafegu a'erju]
departure	**partida** (f)	[par'tʃida]
arrival	**chegada** (f)	[ʃe'gada]
to arrive (by plane)	**chegar** (vi)	[ʃe'gar]
departure time	**hora** (f) **de partida**	['ɔra de par'tʃida]
arrival time	**hora** (f) **de chegada**	['ɔra de ʃe'gada]
to be delayed	**estar atrasado**	[is'tar atra'zadu]
flight delay	**atraso** (m) **de voo**	[a'trazu de 'vou]
information board	**painel** (m) **de informação**	[paj'nɛw de ĩforma'sãw]
information	**informação** (f)	[ĩforma'sãw]
to announce (vt)	**anunciar** (vt)	[anũ'sjar]
flight (e.g., next ~)	**voo** (m)	['vou]
customs	**alfândega** (f)	[aw'fãdʒiga]
customs officer	**funcionário** (m) **da alfândega**	[fũsjo'narju da aw'fãdʒiga]
customs declaration	**declaração** (f) **alfandegária**	[deklara'sãw awfãde'garja]
to fill out (vt)	**preencher** (vt)	[preẽ'ʃer]
to fill out the declaration	**preencher a declaração**	[preẽ'ʃer a deklara'sãw]
passport control	**controle** (m) **de passaporte**	[kõ'troli de pasa'portʃi]
luggage	**bagagem** (f)	[ba'gaʒẽ]
hand luggage	**bagagem** (f) **de mão**	[ba'gaʒẽ de 'mãw]
luggage cart	**carrinho** (m)	[ka'hiɲu]
landing	**pouso** (m)	['pozu]
landing strip	**pista** (f) **de pouso**	['pista de 'pozu]
to land (vi)	**aterrissar** (vi)	[atehi'sar]
airstair (passenger stair)	**escada** (f) **de avião**	[is'kada de a'vjãw]
check-in	**check-in** (m)	[ʃɛ'kin]
check-in counter	**balcão** (m) **do check-in**	[baw'kãw du ʃɛ'kin]

to check-in (vi)	**fazer o check-in**	[fa'zer u ʃɛ'kin]
boarding pass	**cartão** (m) **de embarque**	[kar'tãw de ẽ'barki]
departure gate	**portão** (m) **de embarque**	[por'tãw de ẽ'barki]

transit	**trânsito** (m)	['trãzitu]
to wait (vt)	**esperar** (vt)	[ispe'rar]
departure lounge	**sala** (f) **de espera**	['sala de is'pɛra]
to see off	**despedir-se de ...**	[dʒispe'dʒirsi de]
to say goodbye	**despedir-se** (vr)	[dʒispe'dʒirsi]

24. Airplane

airplane	**avião** (m)	[a'vjãw]
air ticket	**passagem** (f) **aérea**	[pa'saʒẽ a'erja]
airline	**companhia** (f) **aérea**	[kõpa'ɲia a'erja]
airport	**aeroporto** (m)	[aero'portu]
supersonic (adj)	**supersônico**	[super'soniku]

captain	**comandante** (m) **do avião**	[komã'dãtʃi du a'vjãw]
crew	**tripulação** (f)	[tripula'sãw]
pilot	**piloto** (m)	[pi'lotu]
flight attendant (fem.)	**aeromoça** (f)	[aero'mosa]
navigator	**copiloto** (m)	[kopi'lotu]

wings	**asas** (f pl)	['azas]
tail	**cauda** (f)	['kawda]
cockpit	**cabine** (f)	[ka'bini]
engine	**motor** (m)	[mo'tor]
undercarriage (landing gear)	**trem** (m) **de pouso**	[trẽj de 'pozu]
turbine	**turbina** (f)	[tur'bina]

propeller	**hélice** (f)	['ɛlisi]
black box	**caixa-preta** (f)	['kaɪʃa 'preta]
yoke (control column)	**coluna** (f) **de controle**	[ko'luna de kõ'troli]
fuel	**combustível** (m)	[kõbus'tʃivew]

safety card	**instruções** (f pl) **de segurança**	[ĩstru'sõjs de segu'rãsa]
oxygen mask	**máscara** (f) **de oxigênio**	['maskara de oksi'ʒenju]
uniform	**uniforme** (m)	[uni'fɔrmi]
life vest	**colete** (m) **salva-vidas**	[ko'letʃi 'sawva 'vidas]
parachute	**paraquedas** (m)	[para'kɛdas]

takeoff	**decolagem** (f)	[deko'laʒẽ]
to take off (vi)	**descolar** (vi)	[dʒisko'lar]
runway	**pista** (f) **de decolagem**	['pista de deko'laʒẽ]

visibility	**visibilidade** (f)	[vizibili'dadʒi]
flight (act of flying)	**voo** (m)	['vou]

| altitude | altura (f) | [aw'tura] |
| air pocket | poço (m) de ar | ['posu de 'ar] |

seat	assento (m)	[a'sẽtu]
headphones	fone (m) de ouvido	['fɔni de o'vidu]
folding tray (tray table)	mesa (f) retrátil	['meza he'tratʃiw]
airplane window	janela (f)	[ʒa'nɛla]
aisle	corredor (m)	[kohe'dor]

25. Train

train	trem (m)	[trẽj]
commuter train	trem (m) elétrico	[trẽj e'lɛtriku]
express train	trem (m)	[trẽj]
diesel locomotive	locomotiva (f) diesel	[lokomo'tʃiva 'dʒizew]
steam locomotive	locomotiva (f) a vapor	[lokomo'tʃiva a va'por]

| passenger car | vagão (f) de passageiros | [va'gãw de pasa'ʒejrus] |
| dining car | vagão-restaurante (m) | [va'gãw-hestaw'rãtʃi] |

rails	carris (m pl)	[ka'his]
railroad	estrada (f) de ferro	[is'trada de 'fɛhu]
railway tie	travessa (f)	[tra'vɛsa]

platform (railway ~)	plataforma (f)	[plata'fɔrma]
track (~ 1, 2, etc.)	linha (f)	['liɲa]
semaphore	semáforo (m)	[se'maforu]
station	estação (f)	[ista'sãw]

engineer (train driver)	maquinista (m)	[maki'nista]
porter (of luggage)	bagageiro (m)	[baga'ʒejru]
car attendant	hospedeiro, -a (m, f)	[ospe'dejru, -a]
passenger	passageiro (m)	[pasa'ʒejru]
conductor (ticket inspector)	revisor (m)	[hevi'zor]

| corridor (in train) | corredor (m) | [kohe'dor] |
| emergency brake | freio (m) de emergência | ['freju de imer'ʒẽsja] |

compartment	compartimento (m)	[kõpartʃi'mẽtu]
berth	cama (f)	['kama]
upper berth	cama (f) de cima	['kama de 'sima]
lower berth	cama (f) de baixo	['kama de 'baɪʃu]
bed linen, bedding	roupa (f) de cama	['hopa de 'kama]

ticket	passagem (f)	[pa'saʒẽ]
schedule	horário (m)	[o'rarju]
information display	painel (m) de informação	[paj'nɛw de ĩforma'sãw]
to leave, to depart	partir (vt)	[par'tʃir]
departure (of train)	partida (f)	[par'tʃida]

| to arrive (ab. train) | chegar (vi) | [ʃe'gar] |
| arrival | chegada (f) | [ʃe'gada] |

to arrive by train	chegar de trem	[ʃe'gar de trẽj]
to get on the train	pegar o trem	[pe'gar u trẽj]
to get off the train	descer de trem	[de'ser de trẽj]

train wreck	acidente (m) ferroviário	[asi'dẽtʃi feho'vjarju]
to derail (vi)	descarrilar (vi)	[dʒiskahi'ʎar]
steam locomotive	locomotiva (f) a vapor	[lokomo'tʃiva a va'por]
stoker, fireman	foguista (m)	[fo'gista]
firebox	fornalha (f)	[for'naʎa]
coal	carvão (m)	[kar'vãw]

26. Ship

| ship | navio (m) | [na'viu] |
| vessel | embarcação (f) | [ẽbarka'sãw] |

steamship	barco (m) a vapor	['barku a va'por]
riverboat	barco (m) fluvial	['barku flu'vjaw]
cruise ship	transatlântico (m)	[trãzat'lãtʃiku]
cruiser	cruzeiro (m)	[kru'zejru]

yacht	iate (m)	['jatʃi]
tugboat	rebocador (m)	[heboka'dor]
barge	barcaça (f)	[bar'kasa]
ferry	ferry (m), balsa (f)	['fɛʀi], ['balsa]

| sailing ship | veleiro (m) | [ve'lejru] |
| brigantine | bergantim (m) | [behgã'tʃĩ] |

| ice breaker | quebra-gelo (m) | ['kɛbra 'ʒelu] |
| submarine | submarino (m) | [subma'rinu] |

boat (flat-bottomed ~)	bote, barco (m)	['botʃi], ['barku]
dinghy (lifeboat)	baleeira (f)	[bale'ejra]
lifeboat	bote (m) salva-vidas	['botʃi 'sawva 'vidas]
motorboat	lancha (f)	['lãʃa]

captain	capitão (m)	[kapi'tãw]
seaman	marinheiro (m)	[mari'ɲejru]
sailor	marujo (m)	[ma'ruʒu]
crew	tripulação (f)	[tripula'sãw]

boatswain	contramestre (m)	[kõtra'mɛstri]
ship's boy	grumete (m)	[gru'mɛtʃi]
cook	cozinheiro (m) de bordo	[kozi'ɲejru de 'bordu]
ship's doctor	médico (m) de bordo	['mɛdʒiku de 'bordu]
deck	convés (m)	[kõ'vɛs]

mast	**mastro** (m)	['mastru]
sail	**vela** (f)	['vɛla]
hold	**porão** (m)	[po'rãw]
bow (prow)	**proa** (f)	['proa]
stern	**popa** (f)	['popa]
oar	**remo** (m)	['hɛmu]
screw propeller	**hélice** (f)	['ɛlisi]

cabin	**cabine** (m)	[ka'bini]
wardroom	**sala** (f) **dos oficiais**	['sala dus ofi'sjajs]
engine room	**sala** (f) **das máquinas**	['sala das 'makinas]
bridge	**ponte** (m) **de comando**	['põtʃi de ko'mãdu]
radio room	**sala** (f) **de comunicações**	['sala de komunika'sõjs]
wave (radio)	**onda** (f)	['õda]
logbook	**diário** (m) **de bordo**	['dʒjarju de 'bɔrdu]

spyglass	**luneta** (f)	[lu'neta]
bell	**sino** (m)	['sinu]
flag	**bandeira** (f)	[bã'dejra]

| hawser (mooring ~) | **cabo** (m) | ['kabu] |
| knot (bowline, etc.) | **nó** (m) | [nɔ] |

| deckrails | **corrimão** (m) | [kohi'mãw] |
| gangway | **prancha** (f) **de embarque** | ['prãʃa de ẽ'barki] |

anchor	**âncora** (f)	['ãkora]
to weigh anchor	**recolher a âncora**	[heko'ʎer a 'ãkora]
to drop anchor	**jogar a âncora**	[ʒo'gar a 'ãkora]
anchor chain	**amarra** (f)	[a'maha]

port (harbor)	**porto** (m)	['portu]
quay, wharf	**cais, amarradouro** (m)	[kajs], [amaha'doru]
to berth (moor)	**atracar** (vi)	[atra'kar]
to cast off	**desatracar** (vi)	[dʒizatra'kar]

trip, voyage	**viagem** (f)	['vjaʒẽ]
cruise (sea trip)	**cruzeiro** (m)	[kru'zejru]
course (route)	**rumo** (m)	['humu]
route (itinerary)	**itinerário** (m)	[itʃine'rarju]

| fairway
(safe water channel) | **canal** (m) **de navegação** | [ka'naw de navega'sãw] |

| shallows | **banco** (m) **de areia** | ['bãku de a'reja] |
| to run aground | **encalhar** (vt) | [ẽka'ʎar] |

storm	**tempestade** (f)	[tẽpes'tadʒi]
signal	**sinal** (m)	[si'naw]
to sink (vi)	**afundar-se** (vr)	[afũ'darse]
Man overboard!	**Homem ao mar!**	['ɔmẽ aw mah]
SOS (distress signal)	**SOS**	[ɛseo'ɛsi]
ring buoy	**boia** (f) **salva-vidas**	['bɔja 'sawva 'vidas]

CITY

27. Urban transportation

bus	ônibus (m)	['onibus]
streetcar	bonde (m) elétrico	['bõdʒi e'lɛtriku]
trolley bus	trólebus (m)	['trɔlebus]
route (of bus, etc.)	rota (f), itinerário (m)	['hɔta], [itʃine'rarju]
number (e.g., bus ~)	número (m)	['numeru]
to go by ...	ir de ...	[ir de]
to get on (~ the bus)	entrar no ...	[ẽ'trar nu]
to get off ...	descer do ...	[de'ser du]
stop (e.g., bus ~)	parada (f)	[pa'rada]
next stop	próxima parada (f)	['prɔsima pa'rada]
terminus	terminal (m)	[termi'naw]
schedule	horário (m)	[o'rarju]
to wait (vt)	esperar (vt)	[ispe'rar]
ticket	passagem (f)	[pa'saʒẽ]
fare	tarifa (f)	[ta'rifa]
cashier (ticket seller)	bilheteiro (m)	[biʎe'tejru]
ticket inspection	controle (m) de passagens	[kõ'troli de pa'saʒãjʃ]
ticket inspector	revisor (m)	[hevi'zor]
to be late (for ...)	atrasar-se (vr)	[atra'zarsi]
to miss (~ the train, etc.)	perder (vt)	[per'der]
to be in a hurry	estar com pressa	[is'tar kõ 'prɛsa]
taxi, cab	táxi (m)	['taksi]
taxi driver	taxista (m)	[tak'sista]
by taxi	de táxi	[de 'taksi]
taxi stand	ponto (m) de táxis	['põtu de 'taksis]
to call a taxi	chamar um táxi	[ʃa'mar ũ 'taksi]
to take a taxi	pegar um táxi	[pe'gar ũ 'taksi]
traffic	tráfego (m)	['trafegu]
traffic jam	engarrafamento (m)	[ẽgahafa'mẽtu]
rush hour	horas (f pl) de pico	['ɔras de 'piku]
to park (vi)	estacionar (vi)	[istasjo'nar]
to park (vt)	estacionar (vt)	[istasjo'nar]
parking lot	parque (m) de estacionamento	['parki de istasjona'mẽtu]

subway	metrô (m)	[me'tro]
station	estação (f)	[ista'sãw]
to take the subway	ir de metrô	[ir de me'tro]
train	trem (m)	[trẽj]
train station	estação (f) de trem	[ista'sãw de trẽj]

28. City. Life in the city

city, town	cidade (f)	[si'dadʒi]
capital city	capital (f)	[kapi'taw]
village	aldeia (f)	[aw'deja]

city map	mapa (m) da cidade	['mapa da si'dadʒi]
downtown	centro (m) da cidade	['sẽtru da si'dadʒi]
suburb	subúrbio (m)	[su'burbju]
suburban (adj)	suburbano	[subur'banu]

outskirts	periferia (f)	[perife'ria]
environs (suburbs)	arredores (m pl)	[ahe'dɔris]
city block	quarteirão (m)	[kwartej'rãw]
residential block (area)	quarteirão (m) residencial	[kwartej'rãw hezidẽ'sjaw]

traffic	tráfego (m)	['trafegu]
traffic lights	semáforo (m)	[se'maforu]
public transportation	transporte (m) público	[trãs'pɔrtʃi 'publiku]
intersection	cruzamento (m)	[kruza'mẽtu]

crosswalk	faixa (f)	['fajʃa]
pedestrian underpass	túnel (m)	['tunew]
to cross (~ the street)	cruzar, atravessar (vt)	[kru'zar], [atrave'sar]
pedestrian	pedestre (m)	[pe'dɛstri]
sidewalk	calçada (f)	[kaw'sada]

bridge	ponte (f)	['põtʃi]
embankment (river walk)	margem (f) do rio	['marʒẽ du 'hiu]
fountain	fonte (f)	['fõtʃi]

allée (garden walkway)	alameda (f)	[ala'meda]
park	parque (m)	['parki]
boulevard	bulevar (m)	[bule'var]
square	praça (f)	['prasa]
avenue (wide street)	avenida (f)	[ave'nida]
street	rua (f)	['hua]
side street	travessa (f)	[tra'vɛsa]
dead end	beco (m) sem saída	['beku sẽ sa'ida]

house	casa (f)	['kaza]
building	edifício, prédio (m)	[edʒi'fisju], ['prɛdʒju]
skyscraper	arranha-céu (m)	[a'haɲa-sɛw]
facade	fachada (f)	[fa'ʃada]

roof	telhado (m)	[te'ʎadu]
window	janela (f)	[ʒa'nɛla]
arch	arco (m)	['arku]
column	coluna (f)	[ko'luna]
corner	esquina (f)	[is'kina]

store window	vitrine (f)	[vi'trini]
signboard (store sign, etc.)	letreiro (m)	[le'trejru]
poster (e.g., playbill)	cartaz (m)	[kar'taz]
advertising poster	cartaz (m) publicitário	[kar'taz publisi'tarju]
billboard	painel (m) publicitário	[paj'nɛw publisi'tarju]

garbage, trash	lixo (m)	['liʃu]
trash can (public ~)	lixeira (f)	[li'ʃejra]
to litter (vi)	jogar lixo na rua	[ʒo'gar 'liʃu na 'hua]
garbage dump	aterro (m) sanitário	[a'tehu sani'tarju]

phone booth	orelhão (m)	[ore'ʎãw]
lamppost	poste (m) de luz	['postʃi de luz]
bench (park ~)	banco (m)	['bãku]

police officer	polícia (m)	[po'lisja]
police	polícia (f)	[po'lisja]
beggar	mendigo, pedinte (m)	[mẽ'dʒigu], [pe'dʒĩtʃi]
homeless (n)	desabrigado (m)	[dʒizabri'gadu]

29. Urban institutions

store	loja (f)	['lɔʒa]
drugstore, pharmacy	drogaria (f)	[droga'ria]
eyeglass store	ótica (f)	['ɔtʃika]
shopping mall	centro (m) comercial	['sẽtru komer'sjaw]
supermarket	supermercado (m)	[supermer'kadu]

bakery	padaria (f)	[pada'ria]
baker	padeiro (m)	[pa'dejru]
pastry shop	pastelaria (f)	[pastela'ria]
grocery store	mercearia (f)	[mersja'ria]
butcher shop	açougue (m)	[a'sogi]

produce store	fruteira (f)	[fru'tejra]
market	mercado (m)	[mer'kadu]

coffee house	cafeteria (f)	[kafete'ria]
restaurant	restaurante (m)	[hestaw'rãtʃi]
pub, bar	bar (m)	[bar]
pizzeria	pizzaria (f)	[pitsa'ria]

hair salon	salão (m) de cabeleireiro	[sa'lãw de kabelej'rejru]
post office	agência (f) dos correios	[a'ʒẽsja dus ko'hejus]

dry cleaners	lavanderia (f)	[lavãde'ria]
photo studio	estúdio (m) fotográfico	[is'tudʒu foto'grafiku]
shoe store	sapataria (f)	[sapata'ria]
bookstore	livraria (f)	[livra'ria]
sporting goods store	loja (f) de artigos esportivos	['lɔʒa de ar'tʃigus ispor'tʃivus]
clothes repair shop	costureira (m)	[kostu'rejra]
formal wear rental	aluguel (m) de roupa	[alu'gɛw de 'hopa]
video rental store	videolocadora (f)	['vidʒju·loka'dɔra]
circus	circo (m)	['sirku]
zoo	jardim (m) zoológico	[ʒar'dʒĩ zo'lɔʒiku]
movie theater	cinema (m)	[si'nɛma]
museum	museu (m)	[mu'zew]
library	biblioteca (f)	[bibljo'tɛka]
theater	teatro (m)	['tʃjatru]
opera (opera house)	ópera (f)	['ɔpera]
nightclub	boate (f)	['bwatʃi]
casino	cassino (m)	[ka'sinu]
mosque	mesquita (f)	[mes'kita]
synagogue	sinagoga (f)	[sina'gɔga]
cathedral	catedral (f)	[kate'draw]
temple	templo (m)	['tẽplu]
church	igreja (f)	[i'greʒa]
college	faculdade (f)	[fakuw'dadʒi]
university	universidade (f)	[universi'dadʒi]
school	escola (f)	[is'kɔla]
prefecture	prefeitura (f)	[prefej'tura]
city hall	câmara (f) municipal	['kamara munisi'paw]
hotel	hotel (m)	[o'tɛw]
bank	banco (m)	['bãku]
embassy	embaixada (f)	[ẽbaj'ʃada]
travel agency	agência (f) de viagens	[a'ʒẽsja de 'vjaʒẽs]
information office	agência (f) de informações	[a'ʒẽsja de ĩforma'sõjs]
currency exchange	casa (f) de câmbio	['kaza de 'kãbju]
subway	metrô (m)	[me'tro]
hospital	hospital (m)	[ospi'taw]
gas station	posto (m) de gasolina	['postu de gazo'lina]
parking lot	parque (m) de estacionamento	['parki de istasjona'mẽtu]

30. Signs

signboard (store sign, etc.)	**letreiro** (m)	[le'trejru]
notice (door sign, etc.)	**aviso** (m)	[a'vizu]
poster	**pôster** (m)	['poster]
direction sign	**placa** (f) **de direção**	['plaka]
arrow (sign)	**seta** (f)	['sɛta]
caution	**aviso** (m), **advertência** (f)	[a'vizu], [adʒiver'tẽsja]
warning sign	**sinal** (m) **de aviso**	[si'naw de a'vizu]
to warn (vt)	**avisar, advertir** (vt)	[avi'zar], [adʒiver'tʃir]
rest day (weekly ~)	**dia** (m) **de folga**	['dʒia de 'fɔwga]
timetable (schedule)	**horário** (m)	[o'rarju]
opening hours	**horário** (m)	[o'rarju]
WELCOME!	**BEM-VINDOS!**	[bẽj 'vĩdu]
ENTRANCE	**ENTRADA**	[ẽ'trada]
EXIT	**SAÍDA**	[sa'ida]
PUSH	**EMPURRE**	[ẽ'puhe]
PULL	**PUXE**	['puʃe]
OPEN	**ABERTO**	[a'bɛrtu]
CLOSED	**FECHADO**	[fe'ʃadu]
WOMEN	**MULHER**	[mu'ʎer]
MEN	**HOMEM**	['ɔmẽ]
DISCOUNTS	**DESCONTOS**	[dʒis'kõtus]
SALE	**SALDOS, PROMOÇÃO**	['sawdus], [promo'sãw]
NEW!	**NOVIDADE!**	[novi'dadʒi]
FREE	**GRÁTIS**	['gratʃis]
ATTENTION!	**ATENÇÃO!**	[atẽ'sãw]
NO VACANCIES	**NÃO HÁ VAGAS**	['nãw a 'vagas]
RESERVED	**RESERVADO**	[hezer'vadu]
ADMINISTRATION	**ADMINISTRAÇÃO**	[adʒiministra'sãw]
STAFF ONLY	**SOMENTE PESSOAL AUTORIZADO**	[sɔ'mẽtʃi pe'swaw awtori'zadu]
BEWARE OF THE DOG!	**CUIDADO CÃO FEROZ**	[kwi'dadu kãw fe'rɔz]
NO SMOKING	**PROIBIDO FUMAR!**	[proi'bidu fu'mar]
DO NOT TOUCH!	**NÃO TOCAR**	['nãw to'kar]
DANGEROUS	**PERIGOSO**	[peri'gozu]
DANGER	**PERIGO**	[pe'rigu]
HIGH VOLTAGE	**ALTA TENSÃO**	['awta tẽ'sãw]
NO SWIMMING!	**PROIBIDO NADAR**	[proi'bidu na'dar]
OUT OF ORDER	**COM DEFEITO**	[kõ de'fejtu]
FLAMMABLE	**INFLAMÁVEL**	[ĩfla'mavew]

FORBIDDEN	**PROIBIDO**	[proi'bidu]
NO TRESPASSING!	**ENTRADA PROIBIDA**	[ẽ'trada proi'bida]
WET PAINT	**CUIDADO TINTA FRESCA**	[kwi'dadu 'tʃĩta 'freska]

31. Shopping

to buy (purchase)	**comprar** (vt)	[kõ'prar]
purchase	**compra** (f)	['kõpra]
to go shopping	**fazer compras**	[fa'zer 'kõpras]
shopping	**compras** (f pl)	['kõpras]

| to be open (ab. store) | **estar aberta** | [is'tar a'bɛrta] |
| to be closed | **estar fechada** | [is'tar fe'ʃada] |

footwear, shoes	**calçado** (m)	[kaw'sadu]
clothes, clothing	**roupa** (f)	['hopa]
cosmetics	**cosméticos** (m pl)	[koz'mɛtʃikus]
food products	**alimentos** (m pl)	[ali'mẽtus]
gift, present	**presente** (m)	[pre'zẽtʃi]

| salesman | **vendedor** (m) | [vẽde'dor] |
| saleswoman | **vendedora** (f) | [vẽde'dora] |

check out, cash desk	**caixa** (f)	['kaɪʃa]
mirror	**espelho** (m)	[is'peʎu]
counter (store ~)	**balcão** (m)	[baw'kãw]
fitting room	**provador** (m)	[prɔva'dor]

to try on	**provar** (vt)	[pro'var]
to fit (ab. dress, etc.)	**servir** (vi)	[ser'vir]
to like (I like ...)	**gostar** (vt)	[gos'tar]

price	**preço** (m)	['presu]
price tag	**etiqueta** (f) **de preço**	[etʃi'keta de 'presu]
to cost (vt)	**custar** (vt)	[kus'tar]
How much?	**Quanto?**	['kwãtu]
discount	**desconto** (m)	[dʒis'kõtu]

inexpensive (adj)	**não caro**	['nãw 'karu]
cheap (adj)	**barato**	[ba'ratu]
expensive (adj)	**caro**	['karu]
It's expensive	**É caro**	[ɛ 'karu]

rental (n)	**aluguel** (m)	[alu'gɛw]
to rent (~ a tuxedo)	**alugar** (vt)	[alu'gar]
credit (trade credit)	**crédito** (m)	['krɛdʒitu]
on credit (adv)	**a crédito**	[a 'krɛdʒitu]

CLOTHING & ACCESSORIES

32. Outerwear. Coats

clothes	roupa (f)	['hopa]
outerwear	roupa (f) exterior	['hopa iste'rjor]
winter clothing	roupa (f) de inverno	['hopa de ĩ'vɛrnu]
coat (overcoat)	sobretudo (m)	[sobri'tudu]
fur coat	casaco (m) de pele	[kaz'aku de 'pɛli]
fur jacket	jaqueta (f) de pele	[ʒa'keta de 'pɛli]
down coat	casaco (m) acolchoado	[ka'zaku akow'ʃwadu]
jacket (e.g., leather ~)	casaco (m), jaqueta (f)	[kaz'aku], [ʒa'keta]
raincoat (trenchcoat, etc.)	impermeável (m)	[ĩper'mjavew]
waterproof (adj)	a prova d'água	[a 'prɔva 'dagwa]

33. Men's & women's clothing

shirt (button shirt)	camisa (f)	[ka'miza]
pants	calça (f)	['kawsa]
jeans	jeans (m)	['dʒins]
suit jacket	paletó, terno (m)	[pale'tɔ], ['tɛrnu]
suit	terno (m)	['tɛrnu]
dress (frock)	vestido (m)	[ves'tʃidu]
skirt	saia (f)	['saja]
blouse	blusa (f)	['bluza]
knitted jacket (cardigan, etc.)	casaco (m) de malha	[ka'zaku de 'maʎa]
jacket (of woman's suit)	casaco, blazer (m)	[ka'zaku], ['blejzer]
T-shirt	camiseta (f)	[kami'zɛta]
shorts (short trousers)	short (m)	['ʃɔrtʃi]
tracksuit	training (m)	['trejnĩŋ]
bathrobe	roupão (m) de banho	[ho'pãw de 'baɲu]
pajamas	pijama (m)	[pi'ʒama]
sweater	suéter (m)	['swɛter]
pullover	pulôver (m)	[pu'lover]
vest	colete (m)	[ko'letʃi]
tailcoat	fraque (m)	['fraki]
tuxedo	smoking (m)	[iz'mokĩs]

uniform	uniforme (m)	[uni'fɔrmi]
workwear	roupa (f) de trabalho	['hopa de tra'baʎu]
overalls	macacão (m)	[maka'kãws]
coat (e.g., doctor's smock)	jaleco (m), bata (f)	[ʒa'lɛku], ['bata]

34. Clothing. Underwear

underwear	roupa (f) íntima	['hopa 'ĩtʃima]
boxers, briefs	cueca boxer (f)	['kwɛka 'bɔkser]
panties	calcinha (f)	[kaw'siɲa]
undershirt (A-shirt)	camiseta (f)	[kami'zɛta]
socks	meias (f pl)	['mejas]

nightdress	camisola (f)	[kami'zɔla]
bra	sutiã (m)	[su'tʃjã]
knee highs (knee-high socks)	meias longas (f pl)	['mejas 'lõgas]

pantyhose	meias-calças (f pl)	['mejas 'kalsas]
stockings (thigh highs)	meias (f pl)	['mejas]
bathing suit	maiô (m)	[ma'jo]

35. Headwear

hat	chapéu (m), touca (f)	[ʃa'pɛw], ['toka]
fedora	chapéu (m) de feltro	[ʃa'pɛw de 'fewtru]
baseball cap	boné (m) de beisebol	[bo'nɛ de bejsi'bɔw]
flatcap	boina (f)	['bojna]

beret	boina (f) francesa	['bojna frã'seza]
hood	capuz (m)	[ka'puz]
panama hat	chapéu panamá (m)	[ʃa'pɛw pana'ma]
knit cap (knitted hat)	touca (f)	['toka]

headscarf	lenço (m)	['lẽsu]
women's hat	chapéu (m) feminino	[ʃa'pɛw femi'ninu]
hard hat	capacete (m)	[kapa'setʃi]
garrison cap	bibico (m)	[bi'biko]
helmet	capacete (m)	[kapa'setʃi]

| derby | chapéu-coco (m) | [ʃa'pɛw 'koku] |
| top hat | cartola (f) | [kar'tɔla] |

36. Footwear

| footwear | calçado (m) | [kaw'sadu] |
| shoes (men's shoes) | botinas (f pl), sapatos (m pl) | [bo'tʃinas], [sapa'tõjs] |

shoes (women's shoes)	**sapatos** (m pl)	[sa'patus]
boots (e.g., cowboy ~)	**botas** (f pl)	['bɔtas]
slippers	**pantufas** (f pl)	[pã'tufas]
tennis shoes (e.g., Nike ~)	**tênis** (m pl)	['tenis]
sneakers	**tênis** (m pl)	['tenis]
(e.g., Converse ~)		
sandals	**sandálias** (f pl)	[sã'dalias]
cobbler (shoe repairer)	**sapateiro** (m)	[sapa'tejru]
heel	**salto** (m)	['sawtu]
pair (of shoes)	**par** (m)	[par]
shoestring	**cadarço** (m)	[ka'darsu]
to lace (vt)	**amarrar os cadarços**	[ama'har us ka'darsus]
shoehorn	**calçadeira** (f)	[kawsa'dejra]
shoe polish	**graxa** (f) **para calçado**	['graʃa 'para kaw'sadu]

37. Personal accessories

gloves	**luva** (f)	['luva]
mittens	**mitenes** (f pl)	[mi'tɛnes]
scarf (muffler)	**cachecol** (m)	[kaʃe'kɔw]
glasses (eyeglasses)	**óculos** (m pl)	['ɔkulus]
frame (eyeglass ~)	**armação** (f)	[arma'sãw]
umbrella	**guarda-chuva** (m)	['gwarda 'ʃuva]
walking stick	**bengala** (f)	[bẽ'gala]
hairbrush	**escova** (f) **para o cabelo**	[is'kova 'para u ka'belu]
fan	**leque** (m)	['lɛki]
tie (necktie)	**gravata** (f)	[gra'vata]
bow tie	**gravata-borboleta** (f)	[gra'vata borbo'leta]
suspenders	**suspensórios** (m pl)	[suspẽ'sɔrjus]
handkerchief	**lenço** (m)	['lẽsu]
comb	**pente** (m)	['pẽtʃi]
barrette	**fivela** (f) **para cabelo**	[fi'vɛla 'para ka'belu]
hairpin	**grampo** (m)	['grãpu]
buckle	**fivela** (f)	[fi'vɛla]
belt	**cinto** (m)	['sĩtu]
shoulder strap	**alça** (f) **de ombro**	['awsa de 'õbru]
bag (handbag)	**bolsa** (f)	['bowsa]
purse	**bolsa, carteira** (f)	['bowsa], [kar'tejra]
backpack	**mochila** (f)	[mo'ʃila]

38. Clothing. Miscellaneous

fashion	**moda** (f)	['mɔda]
in vogue (adj)	**na moda**	[na 'mɔda]
fashion designer	**estilista** (m)	[istʃi'lista]

collar	**colarinho** (m)	[kola'riɲu]
pocket	**bolso** (m)	['bowsu]
pocket (as adj)	**de bolso**	[de 'bowsu]
sleeve	**manga** (f)	['mãga]
hanging loop	**ganchinho** (m)	[gã'ʃiɲu]
fly (on trousers)	**bragueta** (f)	[bra'gwetʃi]

zipper (fastener)	**zíper** (m)	['ziper]
fastener	**colchete** (m)	[kow'ʃetʃi]
button	**botão** (m)	[bo'tãw]
buttonhole	**botoeira** (f)	[bo'twejra]
to come off (ab. button)	**soltar-se** (vr)	[sow'tarsi]

to sew (vi, vt)	**costurar** (vi)	[kostu'rar]
to embroider (vi, vt)	**bordar** (vt)	[bor'dar]
embroidery	**bordado** (m)	[bor'dadu]
sewing needle	**agulha** (f)	[a'guʎa]
thread	**fio, linha** (f)	['fiu], ['liɲa]
seam	**costura** (f)	[kos'tura]

to get dirty (vi)	**sujar-se** (vr)	[su'ʒarsi]
stain (mark, spot)	**mancha** (f)	['mãʃa]
to crease, crumple (vi)	**amarrotar-se** (vr)	[amaho'tarse]
to tear, to rip (vt)	**rasgar** (vt)	[haz'gar]
clothes moth	**traça** (f)	['trasa]

39. Personal care. Cosmetics

toothpaste	**pasta** (f) **de dente**	['pasta de 'dẽtʃi]
toothbrush	**escova** (f) **de dente**	[is'kova de 'dẽtʃi]
to brush one's teeth	**escovar os dentes**	[isko'var us 'dẽtʃis]

razor	**gilete** (f)	[ʒi'lɛtʃi]
shaving cream	**creme** (m) **de barbear**	['krɛmi de bar'bjar]
to shave (vi)	**barbear-se** (vr)	[bar'bjarsi]

soap	**sabonete** (m)	[sabo'netʃi]
shampoo	**xampu** (m)	[ʃã'pu]

scissors	**tesoura** (f)	[te'zora]
nail file	**lixa** (f) **de unhas**	['liʃa de 'uɲas]
nail clippers	**corta-unhas** (m)	['kɔrta 'uɲas]
tweezers	**pinça** (f)	['pĩsa]

cosmetics	cosméticos (m pl)	[koz'mɛtʃikus]
face mask	máscara (f)	['maskara]
manicure	manicure (f)	[mani'kuri]
to have a manicure	fazer as unhas	[fa'zer as 'uɲas]
pedicure	pedicure (f)	[pedi'kure]

make-up bag	bolsa (f) de maquiagem	['bowsa de ma'kjaʒẽ]
face powder	pó (m)	[pɔ]
powder compact	pó (m) compacto	[pɔ kõ'paktu]
blusher	blush (m)	[blaʃ]

perfume (bottled)	perfume (m)	[per'fumi]
toilet water (lotion)	água-de-colônia (f)	['agwa de ko'lonja]
lotion	loção (f)	[lo'sãw]
cologne	colônia (f)	[ko'lonja]

eyeshadow	sombra (f) de olhos	['sõbra de 'oʎus]
eyeliner	delineador (m)	[delinja'dor]
mascara	máscara (f), rímel (m)	['maskara], ['himew]

lipstick	batom (m)	['batõ]
nail polish, enamel	esmalte (m)	[iz'mawtʃi]
hair spray	laquê (m), spray fixador (m)	[la'ke], [is'prej fiksa'dor]
deodorant	desodorante (m)	[dʒizodo'rãtʃi]

cream	creme (m)	['krɛmi]
face cream	creme (m) de rosto	['krɛmi de 'hostu]
hand cream	creme (m) de mãos	['krɛmi de 'mãws]
anti-wrinkle cream	creme (m) antirrugas	['krɛmi ãtʃi'hugas]
day cream	creme (m) de dia	['krɛmi de 'dʒia]
night cream	creme (m) de noite	['krɛmi de 'nojtʃi]
day (as adj)	de dia	[de 'dʒia]
night (as adj)	da noite	[da 'nojtʃi]

tampon	absorvente (m) interno	[absor'vẽtʃi ĩ'tɛrnu]
toilet paper (toilet roll)	papel (m) higiênico	[pa'pɛw i'ʒjeniku]
hair dryer	secador (m) de cabelo	[seka'dor de ka'belu]

40. Watches. Clocks

watch (wristwatch)	relógio (m) de pulso	[he'lɔʒu de 'puwsu]
dial	mostrador (m)	[mostra'dor]
hand (of clock, watch)	ponteiro (m)	[põ'tejru]
metal watch band	bracelete (f) em aço	[brase'letʃi ẽ 'asu]
watch strap	bracelete (f) em couro	[brase'letʃi ẽ 'koru]

battery	pilha (f)	['piʎa]
to be dead (battery)	acabar (vi)	[aka'bar]
to change a battery	trocar a pilha	[tro'kar a 'piʎa]

| to run fast | estar adiantado | [is'tar adʒjã'tadu] |
| to run slow | estar atrasado | [is'tar atra'zadu] |

wall clock	relógio (m) de parede	[he'lɔʒu de pa'redʒi]
hourglass	ampulheta (f)	[ãpu'ʎeta]
sundial	relógio (m) de sol	[he'lɔʒu de sɔw]
alarm clock	despertador (m)	[dʒisperta'dor]
watchmaker	relojoeiro (m)	[helo'ʒwejru]
to repair (vt)	reparar (vt)	[hepa'rar]

EVERYDAY EXPERIENCE

41. Money

money	dinheiro (m)	[dʒi'ɲejru]
currency exchange	câmbio (m)	['kãbju]
exchange rate	taxa (f) de câmbio	['taʃa de 'kãbju]
ATM	caixa (m) eletrônico	['kaɪʃa ele'troniku]
coin	moeda (f)	['mwɛda]
dollar	dólar (m)	['dɔlar]
euro	euro (m)	['ewru]
lira	lira (f)	['lira]
Deutschmark	marco (m)	['marku]
franc	franco (m)	['frãku]
pound sterling	libra (f) esterlina	['libra ister'linu]
yen	iene (m)	['jɛni]
debt	dívida (f)	['dʒivida]
debtor	devedor (m)	[deve'dor]
to lend (money)	emprestar (vt)	[ẽpres'tar]
to borrow (vi, vt)	pedir emprestado	[pe'dʒir ẽpres'tadu]
bank	banco (m)	['bãku]
account	conta (f)	['kõta]
to deposit (vt)	depositar (vt)	[depozi'tar]
to deposit into the account	depositar na conta	[depozi'tar na 'kõta]
to withdraw (vt)	sacar (vt)	[sa'kar]
credit card	cartão (m) de crédito	[kar'tãw de 'krɛdʒitu]
cash	dinheiro (m) vivo	[dʒi'ɲejru 'vivu]
check	cheque (m)	['ʃɛki]
to write a check	passar um cheque	[pa'sar ũ 'ʃɛki]
checkbook	talão (m) de cheques	[ta'lãw de 'ʃɛkis]
wallet	carteira (f)	[kar'tejra]
change purse	niqueleira (f)	[nike'lejra]
safe	cofre (m)	['kɔfri]
heir	herdeiro (m)	[er'dejru]
inheritance	herança (f)	[e'rãsa]
fortune (wealth)	fortuna (f)	[for'tuna]
lease	arrendamento (m)	[ahẽda'mẽtu]
rent (money)	aluguel (m)	[alu'gɛw]

to rent (sth from sb)	alugar (vt)	[alu'gar]
price	preço (m)	['presu]
cost	custo (m)	['kustu]
sum	soma (f)	['sɔma]

to spend (vt)	gastar (vt)	[gas'tar]
expenses	gastos (m pl)	['gastus]
to economize (vi, vt)	economizar (vi)	[ekonomi'zar]
economical	econômico	[eko'nomiku]

to pay (vi, vt)	pagar (vt)	[pa'gar]
payment	pagamento (m)	[paga'mẽtu]
change (give the ~)	troco (m)	['troku]

tax	imposto (m)	[ĩ'postu]
fine	multa (f)	['muwta]
to fine (vt)	multar (vt)	[muw'tar]

42. Post. Postal service

post office	agência (f) dos correios	[a'ʒẽsja dus ko'hejus]
mail (letters, etc.)	correio (m)	[ko'heju]
mailman	carteiro (m)	[kar'tejru]
opening hours	horário (m)	[o'rarju]

letter	carta (f)	['karta]
registered letter	carta (f) registada	['karta heʒis'tada]
postcard	cartão (m) postal	[kar'tãw pos'taw]
telegram	telegrama (m)	[tele'grama]
package (parcel)	encomenda (f)	[ẽko'mẽda]
money transfer	transferência (f) de dinheiro	[trãsfe'rẽsja de dʒi'ɲejru]

to receive (vt)	receber (vt)	[hese'ber]
to send (vt)	enviar (vt)	[ẽ'vjar]
sending	envio (m)	[ẽ'viu]

address	endereço (m)	[ẽde'resu]
ZIP code	código (m) postal	['kɔdʒigu pos'taw]
sender	remetente (m)	[heme'tẽtʃi]
receiver	destinatário (m)	[destʃina'tarju]

| name (first name) | nome (m) | ['nɔmi] |
| surname (last name) | sobrenome (m) | [sobri'nɔmi] |

postage rate	tarifa (f)	[ta'rifa]
standard (adj)	ordinário	[ordʒi'narju]
economical (adj)	econômico	[eko'nomiku]
weight	peso (m)	['pezu]
to weigh (~ letters)	pesar (vt)	[pe'zar]

envelope	envelope (m)	[ẽve'lɔpi]
postage stamp	selo (m) postal	['selu pos'taw]
to stamp an envelope	colar o selo	[ko'lar u 'selu]

43. Banking

| bank | banco (m) | ['bãku] |
| branch (of bank, etc.) | balcão (f) | [baw'kãw] |

| bank clerk, consultant | consultor (m) bancário | [kõsuw'tor bã'karju] |
| manager (director) | gerente (m) | [ʒe'rẽtʃi] |

bank account	conta (f)	['kõta]
account number	número (m) da conta	['numeru da 'kõta]
checking account	conta (f) corrente	['kõta ko'hẽtʃi]
savings account	conta (f) poupança	['kõta po'pãsa]

to open an account	abrir uma conta	[a'brir 'uma 'kõta]
to close the account	fechar uma conta	[fe'ʃar 'uma 'kõta]
to deposit into the account	depositar na conta	[depozi'tar na 'kõta]
to withdraw (vt)	sacar (vt)	[sa'kar]

| deposit | depósito (m) | [de'pɔzitu] |
| to make a deposit | fazer um depósito | [fa'zer ũ de'pɔzitu] |

| wire transfer | transferência (f) bancária | [trãsfe'rẽsja bã'karja] |
| to wire, to transfer | transferir (vt) | [trãsfe'rir] |

| sum | soma (f) | ['sɔma] |
| How much? | Quanto? | ['kwãtu] |

| signature | assinatura (f) | [asina'tura] |
| to sign (vt) | assinar (vt) | [asi'nar] |

| credit card | cartão (m) de crédito | [kar'tãw de 'krɛdʒitu] |
| code (PIN code) | senha (f) | ['sɛɲa] |

| credit card number | número (m) do cartão de crédito | ['numeru du kar'tãw de 'krɛdʒitu] |
| ATM | caixa (m) eletrônico | ['kaɪʃa ele'troniku] |

check	cheque (m)	['ʃɛki]
to write a check	passar um cheque	[pa'sar ũ 'ʃɛki]
checkbook	talão (m) de cheques	[ta'lãw de 'ʃɛkis]

loan (bank ~)	empréstimo (m)	[ẽ'prɛstʃimu]
to apply for a loan	pedir um empréstimo	[pe'dʒir ũ ẽ'prɛstʃimu]
to get a loan	obter empréstimo	[ob'ter ẽ'prɛstʃimu]
to give a loan	dar um empréstimo	[dar ũ ẽ'prɛstʃimu]
guarantee	garantia (f)	[garã'tʃia]

44. Telephone. Phone conversation

telephone	telefone (m)	[tele'fɔni]
cell phone	celular (m)	[selu'lar]
answering machine	secretária (f) eletrônica	[sekre'tarja ele'tronika]

to call (by phone)	fazer uma chamada	[fa'zer 'uma ʃa'mada]
phone call	chamada (f)	[ʃa'mada]

to dial a number	discar um número	[dʒis'kar ũ 'numeru]
Hello!	Alô!	[a'lo]
to ask (vt)	perguntar (vt)	[pergũ'tar]
to answer (vi, vt)	responder (vt)	[hespõ'der]

to hear (vt)	ouvir (vt)	[o'vir]
well (adv)	bem	[bẽj]
not well (adv)	mal	[maw]
noises (interference)	ruído (m)	['hwidu]

receiver	fone (m)	['fɔni]
to pick up (~ the phone)	pegar o telefone	[pe'gar u tele'fɔni]
to hang up (~ the phone)	desligar (vi)	[dʒizli'gar]

busy (engaged)	ocupado	[oku'padu]
to ring (ab. phone)	tocar (vi)	[to'kar]
telephone book	lista (f) telefônica	['lista tele'fonika]

local (adj)	local	[lo'kaw]
local call	chamada (f) local	[ʃa'mada lo'kaw]
long distance (~ call)	de longa distância	['de 'lõgu dʒis'tãsja]
long-distance call	chamada (f) de longa distância	[ʃa'mada de 'lõgu dʒis'tãsja]
international (adj)	internacional	[ĩternasjo'naw]
international call	chamada (f) internacional	[ʃa'mada ĩternasjo'naw]

45. Cell phone

cell phone	celular (m)	[selu'lar]
display	tela (f)	['tɛla]
button	botão (m)	[bo'tãw]
SIM card	cartão SIM (m)	[kar'tãw sim]

battery	bateria (f)	[bate'ria]
to be dead (battery)	descarregar-se (vr)	[dʒiskahe'garsi]
charger	carregador (m)	[kahega'dor]

menu	menu (m)	[me'nu]
settings	configurações (f pl)	[kõfigura'sõjs]
tune (melody)	melodia (f)	[melo'dʒia]

to select (vt)	escolher (vt)	[isko'ʎer]
calculator	calculadora (f)	[kawkula'dora]
voice mail	correio (m) de voz	[ko'heju de vɔz]
alarm clock	despertador (m)	[dʒisperta'dor]
contacts	contatos (m pl)	[kõ'tatus]

| SMS (text message) | mensagem (f) de texto | [mẽ'saʒẽ de 'testu] |
| subscriber | assinante (m) | [asi'nãtʃi] |

46. Stationery

| ballpoint pen | caneta (f) | [ka'neta] |
| fountain pen | caneta (f) tinteiro | [ka'neta tʃĩ'tejru] |

pencil	lápis (m)	['lapis]
highlighter	marcador (m) de texto	[marka'dor de 'testu]
felt-tip pen	caneta (f) hidrográfica	[ka'neta idro'grafika]

| notepad | bloco (m) de notas | ['blɔku de 'nɔtas] |
| agenda (diary) | agenda (f) | [a'ʒẽda] |

ruler	régua (f)	['hɛgwa]
calculator	calculadora (f)	[kawkula'dora]
eraser	borracha (f)	[bo'haʃa]
thumbtack	alfinete (m)	[awfi'netʃi]
paper clip	clipe (m)	['klipi]

glue	cola (f)	['kɔla]
stapler	grampeador (m)	[grãpja'dor]
hole punch	furador (m) de papel	[fura'dor de pa'pɛw]
pencil sharpener	apontador (m)	[apõta'dor]

47. Foreign languages

language	língua (f)	['lĩgwa]
foreign (adj)	estrangeiro	[istrã'ʒejru]
foreign language	língua (f) estrangeira	['lĩgwa istrã'ʒejra]
to study (vt)	estudar (vt)	[istu'dar]
to learn (language, etc.)	aprender (vt)	[aprẽ'der]

to read (vi, vt)	ler (vt)	[ler]
to speak (vi, vt)	falar (vi)	[fa'lar]
to understand (vt)	entender (vt)	[ẽtẽ'der]
to write (vt)	escrever (vt)	[iskre'ver]

fast (adv)	rapidamente	[hapida'mẽtʃi]
slowly (adv)	lentamente	[lẽta'mẽtʃi]
fluently (adv)	fluentemente	[fluẽte'mẽtʃi]

rules	regras (f pl)	['hɛgras]
grammar	gramática (f)	[gra'matʃika]
vocabulary	vocabulário (m)	[vokabu'larju]
phonetics	fonética (f)	[fo'nɛtʃika]

textbook	livro (m) didático	['livru dʒi'datʃiku]
dictionary	dicionário (m)	[dʒisjo'narju]
teach-yourself book	manual (m) autodidático	[ma'nwaw awtɔdʒi'datʃiku]
phrasebook	guia (m) de conversação	['gia de kõversa'sãw]

cassette, tape	fita (f) cassete	['fita ka'sɛtʃi]
videotape	videoteipe (m)	[vidʒju'tejpi]
CD, compact disc	CD, disco (m) compacto	['sede], ['dʒisku kõ'paktu]
DVD	DVD (m)	[deve'de]

alphabet	alfabeto (m)	[awfa'bɛtu]
to spell (vt)	soletrar (vt)	[sole'trar]
pronunciation	pronúncia (f)	[pro'nũsja]

accent	sotaque (m)	[so'taki]
with an accent	com sotaque	[kõ so'taki]
without an accent	sem sotaque	[sẽ so'taki]

| word | palavra (f) | [pa'lavra] |
| meaning | sentido (m) | [sẽ'tʃidu] |

course (e.g., a French ~)	curso (m)	['kursu]
to sign up	inscrever-se (vr)	[ĩskre'verse]
teacher	professor (m)	[profe'sor]

translation (process)	tradução (f)	[tradu'sãw]
translation (text, etc.)	tradução (f)	[tradu'sãw]
translator	tradutor (m)	[tradu'tor]
interpreter	intérprete (m)	['ĩ'tɛrpretʃi]

| polyglot | poliglota (m) | [pɔli'glɔta] |
| memory | memória (f) | [me'mɔrja] |

MEALS. RESTAURANT

48. Table setting

spoon	colher (f)	[ko'ʎer]
knife	faca (f)	['faka]
fork	garfo (m)	['garfu]
cup (e.g., coffee ~)	xícara (f)	['ʃikara]
plate (dinner ~)	prato (m)	['pratu]
saucer	pires (m)	['piris]
napkin (on table)	guardanapo (m)	[gwarda'napu]
toothpick	palito (m)	[pa'litu]

49. Restaurant

restaurant	restaurante (m)	[hestaw'rãtʃi]
coffee house	cafeteria (f)	[kafete'ria]
pub, bar	bar (m), cervejaria (f)	[bar], [serveʒa'ria]
tearoom	salão (m) de chá	[sa'lãw de ʃa]
waiter	garçom (m)	[gar'sõ]
waitress	garçonete (f)	[garso'netʃi]
bartender	barman (m)	[bar'mã]
menu	cardápio (m)	[kar'dapju]
wine list	lista (f) de vinhos	['lista de 'viɲus]
to book a table	reservar uma mesa	[hezer'var 'uma 'meza]
course, dish	prato (m)	['pratu]
to order (meal)	pedir (vt)	[pe'dʒir]
to make an order	fazer o pedido	[fa'zer u pe'dʒidu]
aperitif	aperitivo (m)	[aperi'tʃivu]
appetizer	entrada (f)	[ẽ'trada]
dessert	sobremesa (f)	[sobri'meza]
check	conta (f)	['kõta]
to pay the check	pagar a conta	[pa'gar a 'kõta]
to give change	dar o troco	[dar u 'troku]
tip	gorjeta (f)	[gor'ʒeta]

50. Meals

food	comida (f)	[ko'mida]
to eat (vi, vt)	comer (vt)	[ko'mer]
breakfast	café (m) da manhã	[ka'fɛ da ma'ɲã]
to have breakfast	tomar café da manhã	[to'mar ka'fɛ da ma'ɲã]
lunch	almoço (m)	[aw'mosu]
to have lunch	almoçar (vi)	[awmo'sar]
dinner	jantar (m)	[ʒã'tar]
to have dinner	jantar (vi)	[ʒã'tar]
appetite	apetite (m)	[ape'tʃitʃi]
Enjoy your meal!	Bom apetite!	[bõ ape'tʃitʃi]
to open (~ a bottle)	abrir (vt)	[a'brir]
to spill (liquid)	derramar (vt)	[deha'mar]
to spill out (vi)	derramar-se (vr)	[deha'marsi]
to boil (vi)	ferver (vi)	[fer'ver]
to boil (vt)	ferver (vt)	[fer'ver]
boiled (~ water)	fervido	[fer'vidu]
to chill, cool down (vt)	esfriar (vt)	[is'frjar]
to chill (vi)	esfriar-se (vr)	[is'frjarse]
taste, flavor	sabor, gosto (m)	[sa'bor], ['gostu]
aftertaste	fim (m) de boca	[fĩ de 'boka]
to slim down (lose weight)	emagrecer (vi)	[imagre'ser]
diet	dieta (f)	['dʒjɛta]
vitamin	vitamina (f)	[vita'mina]
calorie	caloria (f)	[kalo'ria]
vegetarian (n)	vegetariano (m)	[veʒeta'rjanu]
vegetarian (adj)	vegetariano	[veʒeta'rjanu]
fats (nutrient)	gorduras (f pl)	[gor'duras]
proteins	proteínas (f pl)	[prote'inas]
carbohydrates	carboidratos (m pl)	[karboi'dratus]
slice (of lemon, ham)	fatia (f)	[fa'tʃia]
piece (of cake, pie)	pedaço (m)	[pe'dasu]
crumb	migalha (f), farelo (m)	[mi'gaʎa], [fa'rɛlu]
(of bread, cake, etc.)		

51. Cooked dishes

course, dish	prato (m)	['pratu]
cuisine	cozinha (f)	[ko'ziɲa]
recipe	receita (f)	[he'sejta]
portion	porção (f)	[por'sãw]

| salad | salada (f) | [sa'lada] |
| soup | sopa (f) | ['sopa] |

clear soup (broth)	caldo (m)	['kawdu]
sandwich (bread)	sanduíche (m)	[sand'wiʃi]
fried eggs	ovos (m pl) fritos	['ɔvus 'fritus]

| hamburger (beefburger) | hambúrguer (m) | [ã'burger] |
| beefsteak | bife (m) | ['bifi] |

side dish	acompanhamento (m)	[akõpaɲa'mẽtu]
spaghetti	espaguete (m)	[ispa'geti]
mashed potatoes	purê (m) de batata	[pu're de ba'tata]
pizza	pizza (f)	['pitsa]
porridge (oatmeal, etc.)	mingau (m)	[mĩ'gaw]
omelet	omelete (f)	[ome'letʃi]

boiled (e.g., ~ beef)	fervido	[fer'vidu]
smoked (adj)	defumado	[defu'madu]
fried (adj)	frito	['fritu]
dried (adj)	seco	['seku]
frozen (adj)	congelado	[kõʒe'ladu]
pickled (adj)	em conserva	[ẽ kõ'serva]

sweet (sugary)	doce	['dosi]
salty (adj)	salgado	[saw'gadu]
cold (adj)	frio	['friu]
hot (adj)	quente	['kẽtʃi]
bitter (adj)	amargo	[a'margu]
tasty (adj)	gostoso	[gos'tozu]

to cook in boiling water	cozinhar em água fervente	[kozi'ɲar ẽ 'agwa fer'vẽtʃi]
to cook (dinner)	preparar (vt)	[prepa'rar]
to fry (vt)	fritar (vt)	[fri'tar]
to heat up (food)	aquecer (vt)	[ake'ser]

to salt (vt)	salgar (vt)	[saw'gar]
to pepper (vt)	apimentar (vt)	[apimẽ'tar]
to grate (vt)	ralar (vt)	[ha'lar]
peel (n)	casca (f)	['kaska]
to peel (vt)	descascar (vt)	[dʒiskas'kar]

52. Food

meat	carne (f)	['karni]
chicken	galinha (f)	[ga'liɲa]
Rock Cornish hen (poussin)	frango (m)	['frãgu]
duck	pato (m)	['patu]

goose	ganso (m)	['gãsu]
game	caça (f)	['kasa]
turkey	peru (m)	[pe'ru]

pork	carne (f) de porco	['karni de 'porku]
veal	carne (f) de vitela	['karni de vi'tɛla]
lamb	carne (f) de carneiro	['karni de kar'nejru]
beef	carne (f) de vaca	['karni de 'vaka]
rabbit	carne (f) de coelho	['karni de ko'eʎu]

sausage (bologna, etc.)	linguiça (f), salsichão (m)	[lĩ'gwisa], [sawsi'ʃãw]
vienna sausage (frankfurter)	salsicha (f)	[saw'siʃa]
bacon	bacon (m)	['bejkõ]
ham	presunto (m)	[pre'zũtu]
gammon	pernil (m) de porco	[per'niw de 'porku]

pâté	patê (m)	[pa'te]
liver	fígado (m)	['figadu]
hamburger (ground beef)	guisado (m)	[gi'zadu]
tongue	língua (f)	['lĩgwa]

egg	ovo (m)	['ovu]
eggs	ovos (m pl)	['ɔvus]
egg white	clara (f) de ovo	['klara de 'ovu]
egg yolk	gema (f) de ovo	['ʒɛma de 'ovu]

fish	peixe (m)	['pejʃi]
seafood	mariscos (m pl)	[ma'riskus]
crustaceans	crustáceos (m pl)	[krus'tasjus]
caviar	caviar (m)	[ka'vjar]

crab	caranguejo (m)	[karã'geʒu]
shrimp	camarão (m)	[kama'rãw]
oyster	ostra (f)	['ostra]
spiny lobster	lagosta (f)	[la'gosta]
octopus	polvo (m)	['powvu]
squid	lula (f)	['lula]

sturgeon	esturjão (m)	[istur'ʒãw]
salmon	salmão (m)	[saw'mãw]
halibut	halibute (m)	[ali'butʃi]

cod	bacalhau (m)	[baka'ʎaw]
mackerel	cavala, sarda (f)	[ka'vala], ['sarda]
tuna	atum (m)	[a'tũ]
eel	enguia (f)	[ẽ'gia]

trout	truta (f)	['truta]
sardine	sardinha (f)	[sar'dʒiɲa]
pike	lúcio (m)	['lusju]
herring	arenque (m)	[a'rẽki]

bread	**pão** (m)	[pãw]
cheese	**queijo** (m)	['kejʒu]
sugar	**açúcar** (m)	[a'sukar]
salt	**sal** (m)	[saw]
rice	**arroz** (m)	[a'hoz]
pasta (macaroni)	**massas** (f pl)	['masas]
noodles	**talharim, miojo** (m)	[taʎa'rĩ], [mi'oʒu]
butter	**manteiga** (f)	[mã'tejga]
vegetable oil	**óleo** (m) **vegetal**	['ɔlju veʒe'taw]
sunflower oil	**óleo** (m) **de girassol**	['ɔlju de ʒira'sɔw]
margarine	**margarina** (f)	[marga'rina]
olives	**azeitonas** (f pl)	[azej'tɔnas]
olive oil	**azeite** (m)	[a'zejtʃi]
milk	**leite** (m)	['lejtʃi]
condensed milk	**leite** (m) **condensado**	['lejtʃi kõdẽ'sadu]
yogurt	**iogurte** (m)	[jo'gurtʃi]
sour cream	**creme azedo** (m)	['krɛmi a'zedu]
cream (of milk)	**creme** (m) **de leite**	['krɛmi de 'lejtʃi]
mayonnaise	**maionese** (f)	[majo'nɛzi]
buttercream	**creme** (m)	['krɛmi]
groats (barley ~, etc.)	**grãos** (m pl) **de cereais**	['grãws de se'rjajs]
flour	**farinha** (f)	[fa'riɲa]
canned food	**enlatados** (m pl)	[ẽla'tadus]
cornflakes	**flocos** (m pl) **de milho**	['flɔkus de 'miʎu]
honey	**mel** (m)	[mɛw]
jam	**geleia** (m)	[ʒe'lɛja]
chewing gum	**chiclete** (m)	[ʃi'klɛtʃi]

53. Drinks

water	**água** (f)	['agwa]
drinking water	**água** (f) **potável**	['agwa pu'tavɛw]
mineral water	**água** (f) **mineral**	['agwa mine'raw]
still (adj)	**sem gás**	[sẽ gajs]
carbonated (adj)	**gaseificada**	[gazejfi'kadu]
sparkling (adj)	**com gás**	[kõ gajs]
ice	**gelo** (m)	['ʒelu]
with ice	**com gelo**	[kõ 'ʒelu]
non-alcoholic (adj)	**não alcoólico**	[nãw aw'kɔliku]
soft drink	**refrigerante** (m)	[hefriʒe'rãtʃi]
refreshing drink	**refresco** (m)	[he'fresku]

lemonade	**limonada** (f)	[limo'nada]
liquors	**bebidas** (f pl) **alcoólicas**	[be'bidas aw'kɔlikas]
wine	**vinho** (m)	['viɲu]
white wine	**vinho** (m) **branco**	['viɲu 'brãku]
red wine	**vinho** (m) **tinto**	['viɲu 'tʃĩtu]
liqueur	**licor** (m)	[li'kor]
champagne	**champanhe** (m)	[ʃã'paɲi]
vermouth	**vermute** (m)	[ver'mutʃi]
whiskey	**uísque** (m)	['wiski]
vodka	**vodca** (f)	['vodʒka]
gin	**gim** (m)	[ʒĩ]
cognac	**conhaque** (m)	[ko'ɲaki]
rum	**rum** (m)	[hũ]
coffee	**café** (m)	[ka'fɛ]
black coffee	**café** (m) **preto**	[ka'fɛ 'pretu]
coffee with milk	**café** (m) **com leite**	[ka'fɛ kõ 'lejtʃi]
cappuccino	**cappuccino** (m)	[kapu'tʃinu]
instant coffee	**café** (m) **solúvel**	[ka'fɛ so'luvew]
milk	**leite** (m)	['lejtʃi]
cocktail	**coquetel** (m)	[koke'tɛw]
milkshake	**batida** (f), **milkshake** (m)	[ba'tʃida], ['milkʃejk]
juice	**suco** (m)	['suku]
tomato juice	**suco** (m) **de tomate**	['suku de to'matʃi]
orange juice	**suco** (m) **de laranja**	['suku de la'rãʒa]
freshly squeezed juice	**suco** (m) **fresco**	['suku 'fresku]
beer	**cerveja** (f)	[ser'veʒa]
light beer	**cerveja** (f) **clara**	[ser'veʒa 'klara]
dark beer	**cerveja** (f) **preta**	[ser'veʒa 'preta]
tea	**chá** (m)	[ʃa]
black tea	**chá** (m) **preto**	[ʃa 'pretu]
green tea	**chá** (m) **verde**	[ʃa 'verdʒi]

54. Vegetables

vegetables	**vegetais** (m pl)	[veʒe'tajs]
greens	**verdura** (f)	[ver'dura]
tomato	**tomate** (m)	[to'matʃi]
cucumber	**pepino** (m)	[pe'pinu]
carrot	**cenoura** (f)	[se'nora]
potato	**batata** (f)	[ba'tata]
onion	**cebola** (f)	[se'bola]
garlic	**alho** (m)	['aʎu]

cabbage	couve (f)	['kovi]
cauliflower	couve-flor (f)	['kovi 'flɔr]
Brussels sprouts	couve-de-bruxelas (f)	['kovi de bru'ʃelas]
broccoli	brócolis (m pl)	['brɔkolis]

beet	beterraba (f)	[bete'haba]
eggplant	berinjela (f)	[berĩ'ʒɛla]
zucchini	abobrinha (f)	[abo'briɲa]
pumpkin	abóbora (f)	[a'bɔbora]
turnip	nabo (m)	['nabu]

parsley	salsa (f)	['sawsa]
dill	endro, aneto (m)	['ẽdru], [a'netu]
lettuce	alface (f)	[aw'fasi]
celery	aipo (m)	['ajpu]
asparagus	aspargo (m)	[as'pargu]
spinach	espinafre (m)	[ispi'nafri]

pea	ervilha (f)	[er'viʎa]
beans	feijão (m)	[fej'ʒãw]
corn (maize)	milho (m)	['miʎu]
kidney bean	feijão (m) roxo	[fej'ʒãw 'hoʃu]

bell pepper	pimentão (m)	[pimẽ'tãw]
radish	rabanete (m)	[haba'netʃi]
artichoke	alcachofra (f)	[awka'ʃofra]

55. Fruits. Nuts

fruit	fruta (f)	['fruta]
apple	maçã (f)	[ma'sã]
pear	pera (f)	['pera]
lemon	limão (m)	[li'mãw]
orange	laranja (f)	[la'rãʒa]
strawberry (garden ~)	morango (m)	[mo'rãgu]

mandarin	tangerina (f)	[tãʒe'rina]
plum	ameixa (f)	[a'mejʃa]
peach	pêssego (m)	['pesegu]
apricot	damasco (m)	[da'masku]
raspberry	framboesa (f)	[frãbo'eza]
pineapple	abacaxi (m)	[abaka'ʃi]

banana	banana (f)	[ba'nana]
watermelon	melancia (f)	[melã'sia]
grape	uva (f)	['uva]
sour cherry	ginja (f)	['ʒĩʒa]
sweet cherry	cereja (f)	[se'reʒa]
melon	melão (m)	[me'lãw]
grapefruit	toranja (f)	[to'rãʒa]

avocado	**abacate** (m)	[aba'katʃi]
papaya	**mamão** (m)	[ma'mãw]
mango	**manga** (f)	['mãga]
pomegranate	**romã** (f)	['homa]

redcurrant	**groselha** (f) **vermelha**	[[gro'zɛʎa ver'meʎa]
blackcurrant	**groselha** (f) **negra**	[gro'zɛʎa 'negra]
gooseberry	**groselha** (f) **espinhosa**	[gro'zɛʎa ispi'ɲoza]
bilberry	**mirtilo** (m)	[mih'tʃilu]
blackberry	**amora** (f) **silvestre**	[a'mɔra siw'vɛstri]

raisin	**passa** (f)	['pasa]
fig	**figo** (m)	['figu]
date	**tâmara** (f)	['tamara]

peanut	**amendoim** (m)	[amẽdo'ĩ]
almond	**amêndoa** (f)	[a'mẽdwa]
walnut	**noz** (f)	[nɔz]
hazelnut	**avelã** (f)	[ave'lã]
coconut	**coco** (m)	['koku]
pistachios	**pistaches** (m pl)	[pis'taʃis]

56. Bread. Candy

bakers' confectionery (pastry)	**pastelaria** (f)	[pastela'ria]
bread	**pão** (m)	[pãw]
cookies	**biscoito** (m), **bolacha** (f)	[bis'kojtu], [bo'laʃa]

chocolate (n)	**chocolate** (m)	[ʃoko'latʃi]
chocolate (as adj)	**de chocolate**	[de ʃoko'latʃi]
candy (wrapped)	**bala** (f)	['bala]
cake (e.g., cupcake)	**doce** (m), **bolo** (m) **pequeno**	['dosi], ['bolu pe'kenu]
cake (e.g., birthday ~)	**bolo** (m) **de aniversário**	['bolu de aniver'sarju]
pie (e.g., apple ~)	**torta** (f)	['tɔrta]
filling (for cake, pie)	**recheio** (m)	[he'ʃeju]

jam (whole fruit jam)	**geleia** (m)	[ʒe'lɛja]
marmalade	**marmelada** (f)	[marme'lada]
wafers	**wafers** (m pl)	['wafers]
ice-cream	**sorvete** (m)	[sor'vetʃi]
pudding	**pudim** (m)	[pu'dʒĩ]

57. Spices

salt	**sal** (m)	[saw]
salty (adj)	**salgado**	[saw'gadu]

to salt (vt)	salgar (vt)	[saw'gar]
black pepper	pimenta-do-reino (f)	[pi'mẽta-du-hejnu]
red pepper (milled ~)	pimenta (f) vermelha	[pi'mẽta ver'meʎa]
mustard	mostarda (f)	[mos'tarda]
horseradish	raiz-forte (f)	[ha'iz fortʃi]

condiment	condimento (m)	[kõdʒi'mẽtu]
spice	especiaria (f)	[ispesja'ria]
sauce	molho (m)	['moʎu]
vinegar	vinagre (m)	[vi'nagri]

anise	anis (m)	[a'nis]
basil	manjericão (m)	[mãʒeri'kãw]
cloves	cravo (m)	['kravu]
ginger	gengibre (m)	[ʒẽ'ʒibri]
coriander	coentro (m)	[ko'ẽtru]
cinnamon	canela (f)	[ka'nɛla]

sesame	gergelim (m)	[ʒerʒe'lĩ]
bay leaf	folha (f) de louro	['foʎaʃ de 'loru]
paprika	páprica (f)	['paprika]
caraway	cominho (m)	[ko'miɲu]
saffron	açafrão (m)	[asa'frãw]

PERSONAL INFORMATION. FAMILY

58. Personal information. Forms

name (first name)	nome (m)	['nɔmi]
surname (last name)	sobrenome (m)	[sobri'nɔmi]
date of birth	data (f) de nascimento	['data de nasi'mẽtu]
place of birth	local (m) de nascimento	[lo'kaw de nasi'mẽtu]
nationality	nacionalidade (f)	[nasjonali'dadʒi]
place of residence	lugar (m) de residência	[lu'gar de hezi'dẽsja]
country	país (m)	[pa'jis]
profession (occupation)	profissão (f)	[profi'sãw]
gender, sex	sexo (m)	['sɛksu]
height	estatura (f)	[ista'tura]
weight	peso (m)	['pezu]

59. Family members. Relatives

mother	mãe (f)	[mãj]
father	pai (m)	[paj]
son	filho (m)	['fiʎu]
daughter	filha (f)	['fiʎa]
younger daughter	caçula (f)	[ka'sula]
younger son	caçula (m)	[ka'sula]
eldest daughter	filha (f) mais velha	['fiʎa majs 'vɛʎa]
eldest son	filho (m) mais velho	['fiʎu majs 'vɛʎu]
brother	irmão (m)	[ir'mãw]
elder brother	irmão (m) mais velho	[ir'mãw majs 'vɛʎu]
younger brother	irmão (m) mais novo	[ir'mãw majs 'novu]
sister	irmã (f)	[ir'mã]
elder sister	irmã (f) mais velha	[ir'mã majs 'vɛʎa]
younger sister	irmã (f) mais nova	[ir'mã majs 'nɔva]
cousin (masc.)	primo (m)	['primu]
cousin (fem.)	prima (f)	['prima]
mom, mommy	mamãe (f)	[ma'mãj]
dad, daddy	papai (m)	[pa'paj]
parents	pais (pl)	['pajs]
child	criança (f)	['krjãsa]
children	crianças (f pl)	['krjãsas]

grandmother	**avó** (f)	[a'vo]
grandfather	**avô** (m)	[a'vɔ]
grandson	**neto** (m)	['nɛtu]
granddaughter	**neta** (f)	['nɛta]
grandchildren	**netos** (pl)	['nɛtus]
uncle	**tio** (m)	['tʃiu]
aunt	**tia** (f)	['tʃia]
nephew	**sobrinho** (m)	[so'briɲu]
niece	**sobrinha** (f)	[so'briɲa]
mother-in-law (wife's mother)	**sogra** (f)	['sɔgra]
father-in-law (husband's father)	**sogro** (m)	['sogru]
son-in-law (daughter's husband)	**genro** (m)	['ʒẽhu]
stepmother	**madrasta** (f)	[ma'drasta]
stepfather	**padrasto** (m)	[pa'drastu]
infant	**criança** (f) **de colo**	['krjãsa de 'kɔlu]
baby (infant)	**bebê** (m)	[be'be]
little boy, kid	**menino** (m)	[me'ninu]
wife	**mulher** (f)	[mu'ʎer]
husband	**marido** (m)	[ma'ridu]
spouse (husband)	**esposo** (m)	[is'pozu]
spouse (wife)	**esposa** (f)	[is'poza]
married (masc.)	**casado**	[ka'zadu]
married (fem.)	**casada**	[ka'zada]
single (unmarried)	**solteiro**	[sow'tejru]
bachelor	**solteirão** (m)	[sowtej'rãw]
divorced (masc.)	**divorciado**	[dʒivor'sjadu]
widow	**viúva** (f)	['vjuva]
widower	**viúvo** (m)	['vjuvu]
relative	**parente** (m)	[pa'rẽtʃi]
close relative	**parente** (m) **próximo**	[pa'rẽtʃi 'prosimu]
distant relative	**parente** (m) **distante**	[pa'rẽtʃi dʒis'tãtʃi]
relatives	**parentes** (m pl)	[pa'rẽtʃis]
orphan (boy)	**órfão** (m)	['ɔrfãw]
orphan (girl)	**órfã** (f)	['ɔrfã]
guardian (of a minor)	**tutor** (m)	[tu'tor]
to adopt (a boy)	**adotar** (vt)	[ado'tar]
to adopt (a girl)	**adotar** (vt)	[ado'tar]

60. Friends. Coworkers

friend (masc.)	**amigo** (m)	[a'migu]
friend (fem.)	**amiga** (f)	[a'miga]

| friendship | amizade (f) | [ami'zaʤi] |
| to be friends | ser amigos | [ser a'migus] |

buddy (masc.)	amigo (m)	[a'migu]
buddy (fem.)	amiga (f)	[a'miga]
partner	parceiro (m)	[par'sejru]

chief (boss)	chefe (m)	['ʃɛfi]
superior (n)	superior (m)	[supe'rjor]
owner, proprietor	proprietário (m)	[proprje'tarju]
subordinate (n)	subordinado (m)	[suborʤi'nadu]
colleague	colega (m, f)	[ko'lɛga]

acquaintance (person)	conhecido (m)	[koɲe'sidu]
fellow traveler	companheiro (m) de viagem	[kõpa'ɲejru de 'vjaʒẽ]
classmate	colega (m) de classe	[ko'lɛga de 'klasi]

neighbor (masc.)	vizinho (m)	[vi'ziɲu]
neighbor (fem.)	vizinha (f)	[vi'ziɲa]
neighbors	vizinhos (pl)	[vi'ziɲus]

HUMAN BODY. MEDICINE

61. Head

head	cabeça (f)	[ka'besa]
face	rosto, cara (f)	['hostu], ['kara]
nose	nariz (m)	[na'riz]
mouth	boca (f)	['boka]
eye	olho (m)	['oʎu]
eyes	olhos (m pl)	['oʎus]
pupil	pupila (f)	[pu'pila]
eyebrow	sobrancelha (f)	[sobrã'seʎa]
eyelash	cílio (f)	['silju]
eyelid	pálpebra (f)	['pawpebra]
tongue	língua (f)	['lĩgwa]
tooth	dente (m)	['dẽtʃi]
lips	lábios (m pl)	['labjus]
cheekbones	maçãs (f pl) do rosto	[ma'sãs du 'hostu]
gum	gengiva (f)	[ʒẽ'ʒiva]
palate	palato (m)	[pa'latu]
nostrils	narinas (f pl)	[na'rinas]
chin	queixo (m)	['kejʃu]
jaw	mandíbula (f)	[mã'dʒibula]
cheek	bochecha (f)	[bo'ʃeʃa]
forehead	testa (f)	['tɛsta]
temple	têmpora (f)	['tẽpora]
ear	orelha (f)	[o'reʎa]
back of the head	costas (f pl) da cabeça	['kɔstas da ka'besa]
neck	pescoço (m)	[pes'kosu]
throat	garganta (f)	[gar'gãta]
hair	cabelo (m)	[ka'belu]
hairstyle	penteado (m)	[pẽ'tʃjadu]
haircut	corte (m) de cabelo	['kɔrtʃi de ka'belu]
wig	peruca (f)	[pe'ruka]
mustache	bigode (m)	[bi'gɔdʒi]
beard	barba (f)	['barba]
to have (a beard, etc.)	ter (vt)	[ter]
braid	trança (f)	['trãsa]
sideburns	suíças (f pl)	['swisas]
red-haired (adj)	ruivo	['hwivu]

gray (hair)	**grisalho**	[gri'zaʎu]
bald (adj)	**careca**	[ka'rɛka]
bald patch	**calva** (f)	['kawvu]

| ponytail | **rabo-de-cavalo** (m) | ['habu-de-ka'valu] |
| bangs | **franja** (f) | ['frãʒa] |

62. Human body

| hand | **mão** (f) | [mãw] |
| arm | **braço** (m) | ['brasu] |

finger	**dedo** (m)	['dedu]
toe	**dedo** (m) **do pé**	['dedu du pɛ]
thumb	**polegar** (m)	[pole'gar]
little finger	**dedo** (m) **mindinho**	['dedu mĩ'dʒiɲu]
nail	**unha** (f)	['uɲa]

fist	**punho** (m)	['puɲu]
palm	**palma** (f)	['pawma]
wrist	**pulso** (m)	['puwsu]
forearm	**antebraço** (m)	[ãtʃi'brasu]
elbow	**cotovelo** (m)	[koto'velu]
shoulder	**ombro** (m)	['õbru]

leg	**perna** (f)	['pɛrna]
foot	**pé** (m)	[pɛ]
knee	**joelho** (m)	[ʒo'eʎu]
calf (part of leg)	**panturrilha** (f)	[pãtu'hiʎa]
hip	**quadril** (m)	[kwa'driw]
heel	**calcanhar** (m)	[kawka'ɲar]

body	**corpo** (m)	['korpu]
stomach	**barriga** (f), **ventre** (m)	[ba'higa], ['vẽtri]
chest	**peito** (m)	['pejtu]
breast	**seio** (m)	['seju]
flank	**lado** (m)	['ladu]
back	**costas** (f pl)	['kɔstas]
lower back	**região** (f) **lombar**	[he'ʒjãw lõ'bar]
waist	**cintura** (f)	[sĩ'tura]

navel (belly button)	**umbigo** (m)	[ũ'bigu]
buttocks	**nádegas** (f pl)	['nadegas]
bottom	**traseiro** (m)	[tra'zejru]

beauty mark	**sinal** (m), **pinta** (f)	[si'naw], ['pĩta]
birthmark (café au lait spot)	**sinal** (m) **de nascença**	[si'naw de na'sẽsa]
tattoo	**tatuagem** (f)	[ta'twaʒẽ]
scar	**cicatriz** (f)	[sika'triz]

63. Diseases

sickness	doença (f)	[do'ẽsa]
to be sick	estar doente	[is'tar do'ẽtʃi]
health	saúde (f)	[sa'udʒi]

runny nose (coryza)	nariz (m) escorrendo	[na'riz isko'hẽdu]
tonsillitis	amigdalite (f)	[amigda'litʃi]
cold (illness)	resfriado (m)	[hes'frjadu]
to catch a cold	ficar resfriado	[fi'kar hes'frjadu]

bronchitis	bronquite (f)	[brõ'kitʃi]
pneumonia	pneumonia (f)	[pnewmo'nia]
flu, influenza	gripe (f)	['gripi]

nearsighted (adj)	míope	['miopi]
farsighted (adj)	presbita	[pres'bita]
strabismus (crossed eyes)	estrabismo (m)	[istra'bizmu]
cross-eyed (adj)	estrábico, vesgo	[is'trabiku], ['vezgu]
cataract	catarata (f)	[kata'rata]
glaucoma	glaucoma (m)	[glaw'koma]

stroke	AVC (m), apoplexia (f)	[ave'se], [apople'ksia]
heart attack	ataque (m) cardíaco	[a'taki kar'dʒiaku]
myocardial infarction	enfarte (m) do miocárdio	[ẽ'fartʃi du mjo'kardʒiu]
paralysis	paralisia (f)	[parali'zia]
to paralyze (vt)	paralisar (vt)	[parali'zar]

allergy	alergia (f)	[aler'ʒia]
asthma	asma (f)	['azma]
diabetes	diabetes (f)	[dʒja'bɛtʃis]

toothache	dor (f) de dente	[dor de 'dẽtʃi]
caries	cárie (f)	['kari]

diarrhea	diarreia (f)	[dʒja'hɛja]
constipation	prisão (f) de ventre	[pri'zãw de 'vẽtri]
stomach upset	desarranjo (m) intestinal	[dʒiza'hãʒu ĩtestʃi'naw]
food poisoning	intoxicação (f) alimentar	[ĩtoksika'sãw alimẽ'tar]
to get food poisoning	intoxicar-se	[ĩtoksi'karsi]

arthritis	artrite (f)	[ar'tritʃi]
rickets	raquitismo (m)	[haki'tʃizmu]
rheumatism	reumatismo (m)	[hewma'tʃizmu]
atherosclerosis	arteriosclerose (f)	[arterjoskle'rɔzi]

gastritis	gastrite (f)	[gas'tritʃi]
appendicitis	apendicite (f)	[apẽdʒi'sitʃi]
cholecystitis	colecistite (f)	[kulesis'tʃitʃi]
ulcer	úlcera (f)	['uwsera]
measles	sarampo (m)	[sa'rãpu]

rubella (German measles)	rubéola (f)	[hu'bɛola]
jaundice	icterícia (f)	[ikte'risja]
hepatitis	hepatite (f)	[epa'tʃitʃi]

schizophrenia	esquizofrenia (f)	[iskizofre'nia]
rabies (hydrophobia)	raiva (f)	['hajva]
neurosis	neurose (f)	[new'rɔzi]
concussion	contusão (f) cerebral	[kõtu'zãw sere'braw]

cancer	câncer (m)	['kãser]
sclerosis	esclerose (f)	[iskle'rozi]
multiple sclerosis	esclerose (f) múltipla	[iskle'rozi 'muwtʃipla]

alcoholism	alcoolismo (m)	[awko'lizmu]
alcoholic (n)	alcoólico (m)	[aw'kɔliku]
syphilis	sífilis (f)	['sifilis]
AIDS	AIDS (f)	['ajdʒs]

tumor	tumor (m)	[tu'mor]
malignant (adj)	maligno	[ma'lignu]
benign (adj)	benigno	[be'nignu]

fever	febre (f)	['fɛbri]
malaria	malária (f)	[ma'larja]
gangrene	gangrena (f)	[gã'grena]
seasickness	enjoo (m)	[ẽ'ʒou]
epilepsy	epilepsia (f)	[epile'psia]

epidemic	epidemia (f)	[epide'mia]
typhus	tifo (m)	['tʃifu]
tuberculosis	tuberculose (f)	[tuberku'lɔzi]
cholera	cólera (f)	['kɔlera]
plague (bubonic ~)	peste (f) bubônica	['pɛstʃi bu'bonika]

64. Symptoms. Treatments. Part 1

symptom	sintoma (m)	[sĩ'tɔma]
temperature	temperatura (f)	[tẽpera'tura]
high temperature (fever)	febre (f)	['fɛbri]
pulse (heartbeat)	pulso (m)	['puwsu]

dizziness (vertigo)	vertigem (f)	[ver'tʃiʒẽ]
hot (adj)	quente	['kẽtʃi]
shivering	calafrio (m)	[kala'friu]
pale (e.g., ~ face)	pálido	['palidu]

cough	tosse (f)	['tɔsi]
to cough (vi)	tossir (vi)	[to'sir]
to sneeze (vi)	espirrar (vi)	[ispi'har]
faint	desmaio (m)	[dʒiz'maju]

to faint (vi)	desmaiar (vi)	[dʒizma'jar]
bruise (hématome)	mancha (f) preta	['mãʃa 'preta]
bump (lump)	galo (m)	['galu]
to bang (bump)	machucar-se (vr)	[maʃu'karsi]
contusion (bruise)	contusão (f)	[kõtu'zãw]
to get a bruise	machucar-se (vr)	[maʃu'karsi]

to limp (vi)	mancar (vi)	[mã'kar]
dislocation	deslocamento (f)	[dʒizloka'mẽtu]
to dislocate (vt)	deslocar (vt)	[dʒizlo'kar]
fracture	fratura (f)	[fra'tura]
to have a fracture	fraturar (vt)	[fratu'rar]

cut (e.g., paper ~)	corte (m)	['kortʃi]
to cut oneself	cortar-se (vr)	[kor'tarsi]
bleeding	hemorragia (f)	[emoha'ʒia]

| burn (injury) | queimadura (f) | [kejma'dura] |
| to get burned | queimar-se (vr) | [kej'marsi] |

to prick (vt)	picar (vt)	[pi'kar]
to prick oneself	picar-se (vr)	[pi'karsi]
to injure (vt)	lesionar (vt)	[lezjo'nar]
injury	lesão (m)	[le'zãw]
wound	ferida (f), ferimento (m)	[fe'rida], [feri'mẽtu]
trauma	trauma (m)	['trawma]

to be delirious	delirar (vi)	[deli'rar]
to stutter (vi)	gaguejar (vi)	[gage'ʒar]
sunstroke	insolação (f)	[insola'sãw]

65. Symptoms. Treatments. Part 2

| pain, ache | dor (f) | [dor] |
| splinter (in foot, etc.) | farpa (f) | ['farpa] |

sweat (perspiration)	suor (m)	[swor]
to sweat (perspire)	suar (vi)	[swar]
vomiting	vômito (m)	['vomitu]
convulsions	convulsões (f pl)	[kõvuw'sõjs]

pregnant (adj)	grávida	['gravida]
to be born	nascer (vi)	[na'ser]
delivery, labor	parto (m)	['partu]
to deliver (~ a baby)	dar à luz	[dar a luz]
abortion	aborto (m)	[a'bortu]

breathing, respiration	respiração (f)	[hespira'sãw]
in-breath (inhalation)	inspiração (f)	[ĩspira'sãw]
out-breath (exhalation)	expiração (f)	[ispira'sãw]

| to exhale (breathe out) | expirar (vi) | [ispi'rar] |
| to inhale (vi) | inspirar (vi) | [ĩspi'rar] |

disabled person	inválido (m)	[ĩ'validu]
cripple	aleijado (m)	[alej'ʒadu]
drug addict	drogado (m)	[dro'gadu]

deaf (adj)	surdo	['surdu]
mute (adj)	mudo	['mudu]
deaf mute (adj)	surdo-mudo	['surdu-'mudu]

mad, insane (adj)	louco, insano	['loku], [ĩ'sanu]
madman (demented person)	louco (m)	['loku]
madwoman	louca (f)	['loka]
to go insane	ficar louco	[fi'kar 'loku]

gene	gene (m)	['ʒɛni]
immunity	imunidade (f)	[imuni'dadʒi]
hereditary (adj)	hereditário	[eredʒi'tarju]
congenital (adj)	congênito	[kõ'ʒenitu]

virus	vírus (m)	['virus]
microbe	micróbio (m)	[mi'krɔbju]
bacterium	bactéria (f)	[bak'tɛrja]
infection	infecção (f)	[ĩfek'sãw]

66. Symptoms. Treatments. Part 3

| hospital | hospital (m) | [ospi'taw] |
| patient | paciente (m) | [pa'sjẽtʃi] |

diagnosis	diagnóstico (m)	[dʒjag'nɔstʃiku]
cure	cura (f)	['kura]
medical treatment	tratamento (m) médico	[trata'mẽtu 'mɛdʒiku]
to get treatment	curar-se (vr)	[ku'rarsi]
to treat (~ a patient)	tratar (vt)	[tra'tar]
to nurse (look after)	cuidar (vt)	[kwi'dar]
care (nursing ~)	cuidado (m)	[kwi'dadu]

operation, surgery	operação (f)	[opera'sãw]
to bandage (head, limb)	enfaixar (vt)	[ẽfaj'ʃar]
bandaging	enfaixamento (m)	[bã'daʒãj]

vaccination	vacinação (f)	[vasina'sãw]
to vaccinate (vt)	vacinar (vt)	[vasi'nar]
injection, shot	injeção (f)	[inʒe'sãw]
to give an injection	dar uma injeção	[dar 'uma inʒe'sãw]
attack	ataque (m)	[a'taki]
amputation	amputação (f)	[ãputa'sãw]

to amputate (vt)	amputar (vt)	[ãpu'tar]
coma	coma (f)	['kɔma]
to be in a coma	estar em coma	[is'tar ẽ 'kɔma]
intensive care	reanimação (f)	[hianima'sãw]

to recover (~ from flu)	recuperar-se (vr)	[hekupe'rarsi]
condition (patient's ~)	estado (m)	[i'stadu]
consciousness	consciência (f)	[kõ'sjẽsja]
memory (faculty)	memória (f)	[me'mɔrja]

to pull out (tooth)	tirar (vt)	[tʃi'rar]
filling	obturação (f)	[obitura'sãw]
to fill (a tooth)	obturar (vt)	[obitu'rar]

| hypnosis | hipnose (f) | [ip'nɔzi] |
| to hypnotize (vt) | hipnotizar (vt) | [ipnotʃi'zar] |

67. Medicine. Drugs. Accessories

medicine, drug	medicamento (m)	[meʤika'mẽtu]
remedy	remédio (m)	[he'mɛʤju]
to prescribe (vt)	receitar (vt)	[hesej'tar]
prescription	receita (f)	[he'sejta]

tablet, pill	comprimido (m)	[kõpri'midu]
ointment	unguento (m)	[ũ'gwẽtu]
ampule	ampola (f)	[ã'pɔla]
mixture, solution	solução, preparado (m)	[solu'sãw], [prepa'radu]
syrup	xarope (m)	[ʃa'rɔpi]
capsule	cápsula (f)	['kapsula]
powder	pó (m)	[pɔ]

gauze bandage	atadura (f)	[ata'dura]
cotton wool	algodão (m)	[awgo'dãw]
iodine	iodo (m)	['jodu]

| Band-Aid | curativo (m) adesivo | [kura'tivu ade'zivu] |
| eyedropper | conta-gotas (m) | ['kõta 'gotas] |

| thermometer | termômetro (m) | [ter'mometru] |
| syringe | seringa (f) | [se'rĩga] |

| wheelchair | cadeira (f) de rodas | [ka'dejra de 'hɔdas] |
| crutches | muletas (f pl) | [mu'letas] |

painkiller	analgésico (m)	[anaw'ʒɛziku]
laxative	laxante (m)	[la'ʃãtʃi]
spirits (ethanol)	álcool (m)	['awkɔw]
medicinal herbs	ervas (f pl) medicinais	['ɛrvas meʤisi'najs]
herbal (~ tea)	de ervas	[de 'ɛrvas]

APARTMENT

68. Apartment

apartment	**apartamento** (m)	[aparta'mẽtu]
room	**quarto, cômodo** (m)	['kwartu], ['komodu]
bedroom	**quarto** (m) **de dormir**	['kwartu de dor'mir]
dining room	**sala** (f) **de jantar**	['sala de ʒã'tar]
living room	**sala** (f) **de estar**	['sala de is'tar]
study (home office)	**escritório** (m)	[iskri'tɔrju]
entry room	**sala** (f) **de entrada**	['sala de ẽ'trada]
bathroom (room with a bath or shower)	**banheiro** (m)	[ba'ɲejru]
half bath	**lavabo** (m)	[la'vabu]
ceiling	**teto** (m)	['tɛtu]
floor	**chão, piso** (m)	['ʃãw], ['pizu]
corner	**canto** (m)	['kãtu]

69. Furniture. Interior

furniture	**mobiliário** (m)	[mobi'ljarju]
table	**mesa** (f)	['meza]
chair	**cadeira** (f)	[ka'dejra]
bed	**cama** (f)	['kama]
couch, sofa	**sofá, divã** (m)	[so'fa], [dʒi'vã]
armchair	**poltrona** (f)	[pow'trona]
bookcase	**estante** (f)	[is'tãtʃi]
shelf	**prateleira** (f)	[prate'lejra]
wardrobe	**guarda-roupas** (m)	['gwarda 'hopa]
coat rack (wall-mounted ~)	**cabide** (m) **de parede**	[ka'bidʒi de pa'redʒi]
coat stand	**cabideiro** (m) **de pé**	[kabi'dejru de pɛ]
bureau, dresser	**cômoda** (f)	['komoda]
coffee table	**mesinha** (f) **de centro**	[me'ziɲa de 'sẽtru]
mirror	**espelho** (m)	[is'peʎu]
carpet	**tapete** (m)	[ta'petʃi]
rug, small carpet	**tapete** (m)	[ta'petʃi]
fireplace	**lareira** (f)	[la'rejra]
candle	**vela** (f)	['vɛla]

candlestick	castiçal (m)	[kastʃi'saw]
drapes	cortinas (f pl)	[kor'tʃinas]
wallpaper	papel (m) de parede	[pa'pɛw de pa'redʒi]
blinds (jalousie)	persianas (f pl)	[per'sjanas]

table lamp	luminária (f) de mesa	[lumi'narja de 'meza]
wall lamp (sconce)	luminária (f) de parede	[lumi'narja de pa'redʒi]
floor lamp	abajur (m) de pé	[aba'ʒur de 'pɛ]
chandelier	lustre (m)	['lustri]

leg (of chair, table)	pé (m)	[pɛ]
armrest	braço, descanso (m)	['brasu], [dʒis'kãsu]
back (backrest)	costas (f pl)	['kɔstas]
drawer	gaveta (f)	[ga'veta]

70. Bedding

bedclothes	roupa (f) de cama	['hopa de 'kama]
pillow	travesseiro (m)	[trave'sejru]
pillowcase	fronha (f)	['froɲa]
duvet, comforter	cobertor (m)	[kuber'tor]
sheet	lençol (m)	[lẽ'sɔw]
bedspread	colcha (f)	['kowʃa]

71. Kitchen

kitchen	cozinha (f)	[ko'ziɲa]
gas	gás (m)	[gajs]
gas stove (range)	fogão (m) a gás	[fo'gãw a gajs]
electric stove	fogão (m) elétrico	[fo'gãw e'lɛtriku]
oven	forno (m)	['fornu]
microwave oven	forno (m) de micro-ondas	['fornu de mikro'õdas]

refrigerator	geladeira (f)	[ʒela'dejra]
freezer	congelador (m)	[kõʒela'dor]
dishwasher	máquina (f) de lavar louça	['makina de la'var 'losa]

meat grinder	moedor (m) de carne	[moe'dor de 'karni]
juicer	espremedor (m)	[ispreme'dor]
toaster	torradeira (f)	[toha'dejra]
mixer	batedeira (f)	[bate'dejra]

coffee machine	máquina (f) de café	['makina de ka'fɛ]
coffee pot	cafeteira (f)	[kafe'tejra]
coffee grinder	moedor (m) de café	[moe'dor de ka'fɛ]
kettle	chaleira (f)	[ʃa'lejra]
teapot	bule (m)	['buli]

lid	**tampa** (f)	['tãpa]
tea strainer	**coador** (m) **de chá**	[koa'dor de ʃa]
spoon	**colher** (f)	[ko'ʎer]
teaspoon	**colher** (f) **de chá**	[ko'ʎer de ʃa]
soup spoon	**colher** (f) **de sopa**	[ko'ʎer de 'sopa]
fork	**garfo** (m)	['garfu]
knife	**faca** (f)	['faka]
tableware (dishes)	**louça** (f)	['losa]
plate (dinner ~)	**prato** (m)	['pratu]
saucer	**pires** (m)	['piris]
shot glass	**cálice** (m)	['kalisi]
glass (tumbler)	**copo** (m)	['kɔpu]
cup	**xícara** (f)	['ʃikara]
sugar bowl	**açucareiro** (m)	[asuka'rejru]
salt shaker	**saleiro** (m)	[sa'lejru]
pepper shaker	**pimenteiro** (m)	[pimẽ'tejru]
butter dish	**manteigueira** (f)	[mãtej'gejra]
stock pot (soup pot)	**panela** (f)	[pa'nɛla]
frying pan (skillet)	**frigideira** (f)	[friʒi'dejra]
ladle	**concha** (f)	['kõʃa]
colander	**coador** (m)	[koa'dor]
tray (serving ~)	**bandeja** (f)	[bã'deʒa]
bottle	**garrafa** (f)	[ga'hafa]
jar (glass)	**pote** (m) **de vidro**	['pɔtʃi de 'vidru]
can	**lata** (f)	['lata]
bottle opener	**abridor** (m) **de garrafa**	[abri'dor de ga'hafa]
can opener	**abridor** (m) **de latas**	[abri'dor de 'latas]
corkscrew	**saca-rolhas** (m)	['saka-'hoʎas]
filter	**filtro** (m)	['fiwtru]
to filter (vt)	**filtrar** (vt)	[fiw'trar]
trash, garbage (food waste, etc.)	**lixo** (m)	['liʃu]
trash can (kitchen ~)	**lixeira** (f)	[li'ʃejra]

72. Bathroom

bathroom	**banheiro** (m)	[ba'ɲejru]
water	**água** (f)	['agwa]
faucet	**torneira** (f)	[tor'nejra]
hot water	**água** (f) **quente**	['agwa 'kẽtʃi]
cold water	**água** (f) **fria**	['agwa 'fria]
toothpaste	**pasta** (f) **de dente**	['pasta de 'dẽtʃi]

| to brush one's teeth | escovar os dentes | [isko'var us 'dẽtʃis] |
| toothbrush | escova (f) de dente | [is'kova de 'dẽtʃi] |

to shave (vi)	barbear-se (vr)	[bar'bjarsi]
shaving foam	espuma (f) de barbear	[is'puma de bar'bjar]
razor	gilete (f)	[ʒi'lɛtʃi]

to wash (one's hands, etc.)	lavar (vt)	[la'var]
to take a bath	tomar banho	[to'mar baɲu]
shower	chuveiro (m), ducha (f)	[ʃu'vejru], ['duʃa]
to take a shower	tomar uma ducha	[to'mar 'uma 'duʃa]

bathtub	banheira (f)	[ba'ɲejra]
toilet (toilet bowl)	vaso (m) sanitário	['vazu sani'tarju]
sink (washbasin)	pia (f)	['pia]

| soap | sabonete (m) | [sabo'netʃi] |
| soap dish | saboneteira (f) | [sabone'tejra] |

sponge	esponja (f)	[is'põʒa]
shampoo	xampu (m)	[ʃã'pu]
towel	toalha (f)	[to'aʎa]
bathrobe	roupão (m) de banho	[ho'pãw de 'baɲu]

laundry (laundering)	lavagem (f)	[la'vaʒẽ]
washing machine	lavadora (f) de roupas	[lava'dora de 'hopas]
to do the laundry	lavar a roupa	[la'var a 'hopa]
laundry detergent	detergente (m)	[deter'ʒẽtʃi]

73. Household appliances

TV set	televisor (m)	[televi'zor]
tape recorder	gravador (m)	[grava'dor]
VCR (video recorder)	videogravador (m)	['vidʒju·grava'dor]
radio	rádio (m)	['hadʒju]
player (CD, MP3, etc.)	leitor (m)	[lej'tor]

video projector	projetor (m)	[proʒe'tor]
home movie theater	cinema (m) em casa	[si'nɛma ẽ 'kaza]
DVD player	DVD Player (m)	[deve'de 'plejer]
amplifier	amplificador (m)	[ãplifika'dor]
video game console	console (f) de jogos	[kõ'sɔli de 'ʒogus]

video camera	câmera (f) de vídeo	['kamera de 'vidʒju]
camera (photo)	máquina (f) fotográfica	['makina foto'grafika]
digital camera	câmera (f) digital	['kamera dʒiʒi'taw]

vacuum cleaner	aspirador (m)	[aspira'dor]
iron (e.g., steam ~)	ferro (m) de passar	['fɛhu de pa'sar]
ironing board	tábua (f) de passar	['tabwa de pa'sar]

telephone	**telefone** (m)	[tele'fɔni]
cell phone	**celular** (m)	[selu'lar]
typewriter	**máquina** (f) **de escrever**	['makina de iskre'ver]
sewing machine	**máquina** (f) **de costura**	['makina de kos'tura]

microphone	**microfone** (m)	[mikro'fɔni]
headphones	**fone** (m) **de ouvido**	['fɔni de o'vidu]
remote control (TV)	**controle remoto** (m)	[kõ'troli he'mɔtu]

CD, compact disc	**CD** (m)	['sede]
cassette, tape	**fita** (f) **cassete**	['fita ka'sɛtʃi]
vinyl record	**disco** (m) **de vinil**	['dʒisku de vi'niw]

THE EARTH. WEATHER

74. Outer space

space	espaço, cosmo (m)	[is'pasu], ['kɔzmu]
space (as adj)	espacial, cósmico	[ispa'sjaw], ['kɔzmiku]
outer space	espaço (m) cósmico	[is'pasu 'kɔzmiku]
world	mundo (m)	['mũdu]
universe	universo (m)	[uni'vɛrsu]
galaxy	galáxia (f)	[ga'laksja]
star	estrela (f)	[is'trela]
constellation	constelação (f)	[kõstela'sãw]
planet	planeta (m)	[pla'neta]
satellite	satélite (m)	[sa'tɛlitʃi]
meteorite	meteorito (m)	[meteo'ritu]
comet	cometa (m)	[ko'meta]
asteroid	asteroide (m)	[aste'rɔjdʒi]
orbit	órbita (f)	['ɔrbita]
to revolve	girar (vi)	[ʒi'rar]
(~ around the Earth)		
atmosphere	atmosfera (f)	[atmos'fɛra]
the Sun	Sol (m)	[sɔw]
solar system	Sistema (m) Solar	[sis'tɛma so'lar]
solar eclipse	eclipse (m) solar	[e'klipsi so'lar]
the Earth	Terra (f)	['tɛha]
the Moon	Lua (f)	['lua]
Mars	Marte (m)	['martʃi]
Venus	Vênus (f)	['venus]
Jupiter	Júpiter (m)	['ʒupiter]
Saturn	Saturno (m)	[sa'turnu]
Mercury	Mercúrio (m)	[mer'kurju]
Uranus	Urano (m)	[u'ranu]
Neptune	Netuno (m)	[ne'tunu]
Pluto	Plutão (m)	[plu'tãw]
Milky Way	Via Láctea (f)	['via 'laktja]
Great Bear (Ursa Major)	Ursa Maior (f)	[ursa ma'jɔr]
North Star	Estrela Polar (f)	[is'trela po'lar]

Martian	marciano (m)	[mar'sjanu]
extraterrestrial (n)	extraterrestre (m)	[estrate'hɛstri]
alien	alienígena (m)	[alje'niʒena]
flying saucer	disco (m) voador	['dʒisku vwa'dor]

spaceship	nave (f) espacial	['navi ispa'sjaw]
space station	estação (f) orbital	[eʃta'sãw orbi'taw]
blast-off	lançamento (m)	[lãsa'mẽtu]

engine	motor (m)	[mo'tor]
nozzle	bocal (m)	[bo'kaw]
fuel	combustível (m)	[kõbus'tʃivew]

cockpit, flight deck	cabine (f)	[ka'bini]
antenna	antena (f)	[ã'tɛna]
porthole	vigia (f)	[vi'ʒia]
solar panel	bateria (f) solar	[bate'ria so'lar]
spacesuit	traje (m) espacial	['traʒi ispa'sjaw]

| weightlessness | imponderabilidade (f) | [ĩpõderabili'dadʒi] |
| oxygen | oxigênio (m) | [oksi'ʒenju] |

| docking (in space) | acoplagem (f) | [ako'plaʒẽ] |
| to dock (vi, vt) | fazer uma acoplagem | [fa'zer 'uma ako'plaʒẽ] |

observatory	observatório (m)	[observa'tɔrju]
telescope	telescópio (m)	[tele'skɔpju]
to observe (vt)	observar (vt)	[obser'var]
to explore (vt)	explorar (vt)	[isplo'rar]

75. The Earth

the Earth	Terra (f)	['tɛha]
the globe (the Earth)	globo (m) terrestre	['globu te'hɛstri]
planet	planeta (m)	[pla'neta]

atmosphere	atmosfera (f)	[atmos'fɛra]
geography	geografia (f)	[ʒeogra'fia]
nature	natureza (f)	[natu'reza]

globe (table ~)	globo (m)	['globu]
map	mapa (m)	['mapa]
atlas	atlas (m)	['atlas]

Europe	Europa (f)	[ew'rɔpa]
Asia	Ásia (f)	['azja]
Africa	África (f)	['afrika]
Australia	Austrália (f)	[aws'tralja]
America	América (f)	[a'mɛrika]
North America	América (f) do Norte	[a'mɛrika du 'nɔrtʃi]

South America	**América** (f) **do Sul**	[a'mɛrika du suw]
Antarctica	**Antártida** (f)	[ã'tartʃida]
the Arctic	**Ártico** (m)	['artʃiku]

76. Cardinal directions

north	**norte** (m)	['nɔrtʃi]
to the north	**para norte**	['para 'nɔrtʃi]
in the north	**no norte**	[nu 'nɔrtʃi]
northern (adj)	**do norte**	[du 'nɔrtʃi]

south	**sul** (m)	[suw]
to the south	**para sul**	['para suw]
in the south	**no sul**	[nu suw]
southern (adj)	**do sul**	[du suw]

west	**oeste, ocidente** (m)	['wɛstʃi], [osi'dẽtʃi]
to the west	**para oeste**	['para 'wɛstʃi]
in the west	**no oeste**	[nu 'wɛstʃi]
western (adj)	**ocidental**	[osidẽ'taw]

east	**leste, oriente** (m)	['lɛstʃi], [o'rjẽtʃi]
to the east	**para leste**	['para 'lɛstʃi]
in the east	**no leste**	[nu 'lɛstʃi]
eastern (adj)	**oriental**	[orjẽ'taw]

77. Sea. Ocean

sea	**mar** (m)	[mah]
ocean	**oceano** (m)	[o'sjanu]
gulf (bay)	**golfo** (m)	['gowfu]
straits	**estreito** (m)	[is'trejtu]

land (solid ground)	**terra** (f) **firme**	['tɛha 'firmi]
continent (mainland)	**continente** (m)	[kõtʃi'nẽtʃi]
island	**ilha** (f)	['iʎa]
peninsula	**península** (f)	[pe'nĩsula]
archipelago	**arquipélago** (m)	[arki'pɛlagu]

bay, cove	**baía** (f)	[ba'ia]
harbor	**porto** (m)	['portu]
lagoon	**lagoa** (f)	[la'goa]
cape	**cabo** (m)	['kabu]

atoll	**atol** (m)	[a'tɔw]
reef	**recife** (m)	[he'sifi]
coral	**coral** (m)	[ko'raw]
coral reef	**recife** (m) **de coral**	[he'sifi de ko'raw]

deep (adj)	profundo	[pro'fũdu]
depth (deep water)	profundidade (f)	[profũdʒi'dadʒi]
abyss	abismo (m)	[a'bizmu]
trench (e.g., Mariana ~)	fossa (f) oceânica	['fɔsa o'sjanika]

| current (Ocean ~) | corrente (f) | [ko'hẽtʃi] |
| to surround (bathe) | banhar (vt) | [ba'ɲar] |

| shore | litoral (m) | [lito'raw] |
| coast | costa (f) | ['kɔsta] |

flow (flood tide)	maré (f) alta	[ma'rɛ 'awta]
ebb (ebb tide)	refluxo (m)	[he'fluksu]
shoal	restinga (f)	[hes'tʃĩga]
bottom (~ of the sea)	fundo (m)	['fũdu]

wave	onda (f)	['õda]
crest (~ of a wave)	crista (f) da onda	['krista da 'õda]
spume (sea foam)	espuma (f)	[is'puma]

storm (sea storm)	tempestade (f)	[tẽpes'tadʒi]
hurricane	furacão (m)	[fura'kãw]
tsunami	tsunami (m)	[tsu'nami]
calm (dead ~)	calmaria (f)	[kawma'ria]
quiet, calm (adj)	calmo	['kawmu]

| pole | polo (m) | ['pɔlu] |
| polar (adj) | polar | [po'lar] |

latitude	latitude (f)	[latʃi'tudʒi]
longitude	longitude (f)	[lõʒi'tudʒi]
parallel	paralela (f)	[para'lɛla]
equator	equador (m)	[ekwa'dor]

sky	céu (m)	[sɛw]
horizon	horizonte (m)	[ori'zõtʃi]
air	ar (m)	[ar]

lighthouse	farol (m)	[fa'rɔw]
to dive (vi)	mergulhar (vi)	[mergu'ʎar]
to sink (ab. boat)	afundar-se (vr)	[afũ'darse]
treasures	tesouros (m pl)	[te'zorus]

78. Seas' and Oceans' names

Atlantic Ocean	Oceano (m) Atlântico	[o'sjanu at'lãtʃiku]
Indian Ocean	Oceano (m) Índico	[o'sjanu 'ĩdiku]
Pacific Ocean	Oceano (m) Pacífico	[o'sjanu pa'sifiku]
Arctic Ocean	Oceano (m) Ártico	[o'sjanu 'artʃiku]
Black Sea	Mar (m) Negro	[mah 'negru]

Red Sea	Mar (m) Vermelho	[mah ver'meʎu]
Yellow Sea	Mar (m) Amarelo	[mah ama'rɛlu]
White Sea	Mar (m) Branco	[mah 'brãku]

Caspian Sea	Mar (m) Cáspio	[mah 'kaspju]
Dead Sea	Mar (m) Morto	[mah 'mortu]
Mediterranean Sea	Mar (m) Mediterrâneo	[mah medʒite'hanju]

| Aegean Sea | Mar (m) Egeu | [mah e'ʒew] |
| Adriatic Sea | Mar (m) Adriático | [mah a'drjatʃiku] |

Arabian Sea	Mar (m) Arábico	[mah a'rabiku]
Sea of Japan	Mar (m) do Japão	[mah du ʒa'pãw]
Bering Sea	Mar (m) de Bering	[mah de berĩgi]
South China Sea	Mar (m) da China Meridional	[mah da 'ʃina meridʒjo'naw]

Coral Sea	Mar (m) de Coral	[mah de ko'raw]
Tasman Sea	Mar (m) de Tasman	[mah de tazman]
Caribbean Sea	Mar (m) do Caribe	[mah du ka'ribi]

| Barents Sea | Mar (m) de Barents | [mah de barẽts] |
| Kara Sea | Mar (m) de Kara | [mah de 'kara] |

North Sea	Mar (m) do Norte	[mah du 'nɔrtʃi]
Baltic Sea	Mar (m) Báltico	[mah 'bawtʃiku]
Norwegian Sea	Mar (m) da Noruega	[mah da nor'wɛga]

79. Mountains

mountain	montanha (f)	[mõ'taɲa]
mountain range	cordilheira (f)	[kordʒi'ʎejra]
mountain ridge	serra (f)	['sɛha]

summit, top	cume (m)	['kumi]
peak	pico (m)	['piku]
foot (~ of the mountain)	pé (m)	[pɛ]
slope (mountainside)	declive (m)	[de'klivi]

volcano	vulcão (m)	[vuw'kãw]
active volcano	vulcão (m) ativo	[vuw'kãw a'tʃivu]
dormant volcano	vulcão (m) extinto	[vuw'kãw is'tʃĩtu]

eruption	erupção (f)	[erup'sãw]
crater	cratera (f)	[kra'tɛra]
magma	magma (m)	['magma]
lava	lava (f)	['lava]
molten (~ lava)	fundido	[fũ'dʒidu]
canyon	cânion, desfiladeiro (m)	['kanjon], [dʒisfila'dejru]
gorge	garganta (f)	[gar'gãta]

| crevice | fenda (f) | ['fẽda] |
| abyss (chasm) | precipício (m) | [presi'pisju] |

pass, col	passo, colo (m)	['pasu], ['kɔlu]
plateau	planalto (m)	[pla'nawtu]
cliff	falésia (f)	[fa'lɛzja]
hill	colina (f)	[ko'lina]

glacier	geleira (f)	[ʒe'lejra]
waterfall	cachoeira (f)	[kaʃ'wejra]
geyser	gêiser (m)	['ʒɛjzer]
lake	lago (m)	['lagu]

plain	planície (f)	[pla'nisi]
landscape	paisagem (f)	[paj'zaʒẽ]
echo	eco (m)	['ɛku]

alpinist	alpinista (m)	[awpi'nista]
rock climber	escalador (m)	[iskala'dor]
to conquer (in climbing)	conquistar (vt)	[kõkis'tar]
climb (an easy ~)	subida, escalada (f)	[su'bida], [iska'lada]

80. Mountains names

The Alps	Alpes (m pl)	['awpis]
Mont Blanc	Monte Branco (m)	['mõtʃi 'brãku]
The Pyrenees	Pirineus (m pl)	[piri'news]

The Carpathians	Cárpatos (m pl)	['karpatus]
The Ural Mountains	Urais (m pl)	[u'rajs]
The Caucasus Mountains	Cáucaso (m)	['kawkazu]
Mount Elbrus	Elbrus (m)	[el'brus]

The Altai Mountains	Altai (m)	[al'taj]
The Tian Shan	Tian Shan (m)	[tjan ʃan]
The Pamir Mountains	Pamir (m)	[pa'mir]
The Himalayas	Himalaia (m)	[ima'laja]
Mount Everest	monte Everest (m)	['mõtʃi eve'rest]

| The Andes | Cordilheira (f) dos Andes | [kordʒi'ʎejra dus 'ãdʒis] |
| Mount Kilimanjaro | Kilimanjaro (m) | [kilimã'ʒaru] |

81. Rivers

river	rio (m)	['hiu]
spring (natural source)	fonte, nascente (f)	['fõtʃi], [na'sẽtʃi]
riverbed (river channel)	leito (m) de rio	['lejtu de 'hiu]
basin (river valley)	bacia (f)	[ba'sia]

to flow into ...	desaguar no ...	[dʒiza'gwar nu]
tributary	afluente (m)	[a'flwẽtʃi]
bank (of river)	margem (f)	['marʒẽ]

current (stream)	corrente (f)	[ko'hẽtʃi]
downstream (adv)	rio abaixo	['hiu a'baɪʃu]
upstream (adv)	rio acima	['hiu a'sima]

inundation	inundação (f)	[ĩtrodu'sãw]
flooding	cheia (f)	['ʃeja]
to overflow (vi)	transbordar (vi)	[trãzbor'dar]
to flood (vt)	inundar (vt)	[inũ'dar]

| shallow (shoal) | banco (m) de areia | ['bãku de a'reja] |
| rapids | corredeira (f) | [kohe'dejra] |

dam	barragem (f)	[ba'haʒẽ]
canal	canal (m)	[ka'naw]
reservoir (artificial lake)	reservatório (m) de água	[hezerva'tɔrju de 'agwa]
sluice, lock	eclusa (f)	[e'kluza]

water body (pond, etc.)	corpo (m) de água	['korpu de 'agwa]
swamp (marshland)	pântano (m)	['pãtanu]
bog, marsh	lamaçal (m)	[lama'saw]
whirlpool	rodamoinho (m)	[hodamo'iɲu]

stream (brook)	riacho (m)	['hjaʃu]
drinking (ab. water)	potável	[po'tavew]
fresh (~ water)	doce	['dosi]

| ice | gelo (m) | ['ʒelu] |
| to freeze over (ab. river, etc.) | congelar-se (vr) | [kõʒe'larsi] |

82. Rivers' names

| Seine | rio Sena (m) | ['hiu 'sɛna] |
| Loire | rio Loire (m) | ['hiu lu'ar] |

Thames	rio Tâmisa (m)	['hiu 'tamiza]
Rhine	rio Reno (m)	['hiu 'henu]
Danube	rio Danúbio (m)	['hiu da'nubju]

Volga	rio Volga (m)	['hiu 'vɔlga]
Don	rio Don (m)	['hiu dɔn]
Lena	rio Lena (m)	['hiu 'lena]

Yellow River	rio Amarelo (m)	['hiu ama'rɛlu]
Yangtze	rio Yangtzé (m)	['hiu jã'gtzɛ]
Mekong	rio Mekong (m)	['hiu mi'kõg]

Ganges	rio Ganges (m)	['hiu 'gændʒi:z]
Nile River	rio Nilo (m)	['hiu 'nilu]
Congo River	rio Congo (m)	['hiu 'kõgu]
Okavango River	rio Cubango (m)	['hiu ku'bãgu]
Zambezi River	rio Zambeze (m)	['hiu zã'bezi]
Limpopo River	rio Limpopo (m)	['hiu ʎ'popu]
Mississippi River	rio Mississippi (m)	['hiu misi'sipi]

83. Forest

| forest, wood | floresta (f), bosque (m) | [flo'rɛsta], ['bɔski] |
| forest (as adj) | florestal | [flores'taw] |

thick forest	mata (f) fechada	['mata fe'ʃada]
grove	arvoredo (m)	[arvo'redu]
forest clearing	clareira (f)	[kla'rejra]

| thicket | matagal (m) | [mata'gaw] |
| scrubland | mato (m), caatinga (f) | ['matu], [ka'tʃĩga] |

| footpath (troddenpath) | trilha, vereda (f) | ['triʎa], [ve'reda] |
| gully | ravina (f) | [ha'vina] |

tree	árvore (f)	['arvori]
leaf	folha (f)	['foʎa]
leaves (foliage)	folhagem (f)	[fo'ʎaʒẽ]

fall of leaves	queda (f) das folhas	['kɛda das 'foʎas]
to fall (ab. leaves)	cair (vi)	[ka'ir]
top (of the tree)	topo (m)	['topu]

branch	ramo (m)	['hamu]
bough	galho (m)	['gaʎu]
bud (on shrub, tree)	botão (m)	[bo'tãw]
needle (of pine tree)	agulha (f)	[a'guʎa]
pine cone	pinha (f)	['piɲa]

tree hollow	buraco (m) de árvore	[bu'raku de 'arvori]
nest	ninho (m)	['niɲu]
burrow (animal hole)	toca (f)	['tɔka]

trunk	tronco (m)	['trõku]
root	raiz (f)	[ha'iz]
bark	casca (f) de árvore	['kaska de 'arvori]
moss	musgo (m)	['muzgu]

to uproot (remove trees or tree stumps)	arrancar pela raiz	[ahã'kar 'pɛla ha'iz]
to chop down	cortar (vt)	[kor'tar]
to deforest (vt)	desflorestar (vt)	[dʒisflores'tar]

tree stump	toco, cepo (m)	['toku], ['sepu]
campfire	fogueira (f)	[fo'gejra]
forest fire	incêndio (m) florestal	[ĩ'sẽdʒju flores'taw]
to extinguish (vt)	apagar (vt)	[apa'gar]

forest ranger	guarda-parque (m)	['gwarda 'parki]
protection	proteção (f)	[prote'sãw]
to protect (~ nature)	proteger (vt)	[prote'ʒer]
poacher	caçador (m) furtivo	[kasa'dor fur'tʃivu]
steel trap	armadilha (f)	arma'dʒiʎa]

| to gather, to pick (vt) | colher (vt) | [ko'ʎer] |
| to lose one's way | perder-se (vr) | [per'dersi] |

84. Natural resources

natural resources	recursos (m pl) naturais	[he'kursus natu'rajs]
minerals	minerais (m pl)	[mine'rajs]
deposits	depósitos (m pl)	[de'pozitus]
field (e.g., oilfield)	jazida (f)	[ʒa'zida]

to mine (extract)	extrair (vt)	[istra'jir]
mining (extraction)	extração (f)	[istra'sãw]
ore	minério (m)	[mi'nɛrju]
mine (e.g., for coal)	mina (f)	['mina]
shaft (mine ~)	poço (m) de mina	['posu de 'mina]
miner	mineiro (m)	[mi'nejru]

| gas (natural ~) | gás (m) | [gajs] |
| gas pipeline | gasoduto (m) | [gazo'dutu] |

oil (petroleum)	petróleo (m)	[pe'trɔlju]
oil pipeline	oleoduto (m)	[oljo'dutu]
oil well	poço (m) de petróleo	['posu de pe'trɔlju]
derrick (tower)	torre (f) petrolífera	['tohi petro'lifera]
tanker	petroleiro (m)	[petro'lejru]

sand	areia (f)	[a'reja]
limestone	calcário (m)	[kaw'karju]
gravel	cascalho (m)	[kas'kaʎu]
peat	turfa (f)	['turfa]
clay	argila (f)	[ar'ʒila]
coal	carvão (m)	[kar'vãw]

iron (ore)	ferro (m)	['fɛhu]
gold	ouro (m)	['oru]
silver	prata (f)	['prata]
nickel	níquel (m)	['nikew]
copper	cobre (m)	['kɔbri]
zinc	zinco (m)	['zĩku]

manganese	**manganês** (m)	[mãga'nes]
mercury	**mercúrio** (m)	[mer'kurju]
lead	**chumbo** (m)	['ʃũbu]
mineral	**mineral** (m)	[mine'raw]
crystal	**cristal** (m)	[kris'taw]
marble	**mármore** (m)	['marmori]
uranium	**urânio** (m)	[u'ranju]

85. Weather

weather	**tempo** (m)	['tẽpu]
weather forecast	**previsão** (f) **do tempo**	[previ'zãw du 'tẽpu]
temperature	**temperatura** (f)	[tẽpera'tura]
thermometer	**termômetro** (m)	[ter'mometru]
barometer	**barômetro** (m)	[ba'romɛtru]
humid (adj)	**úmido**	['umidu]
humidity	**umidade** (f)	[umi'daʤi]
heat (extreme ~)	**calor** (m)	[ka'lor]
hot (torrid)	**tórrido**	['tɔhidu]
it's hot	**está muito calor**	[is'ta 'mwĩtu ka'lor]
it's warm	**está calor**	[is'ta ka'lor]
warm (moderately hot)	**quente**	['kẽtʃi]
it's cold	**está frio**	[is'ta 'friu]
cold (adj)	**frio**	['friu]
sun	**sol** (m)	[sɔw]
to shine (vi)	**brilhar** (vi)	[bri'ʎar]
sunny (day)	**de sol, ensolarado**	[de sɔw], [ẽsola'radu]
to come up (vi)	**nascer** (vi)	[na'ser]
to set (vi)	**pôr-se** (vr)	['porsi]
cloud	**nuvem** (f)	['nuvẽj]
cloudy (adj)	**nublado**	[nu'bladu]
rain cloud	**nuvem** (f) **preta**	['nuvẽj 'preta]
somber (gloomy)	**escuro**	[is'kuru]
rain	**chuva** (f)	['ʃuva]
it's raining	**está a chover**	[is'ta a ʃo'ver]
rainy (~ day, weather)	**chuvoso**	[ʃu'vozu]
to drizzle (vi)	**chuviscar** (vi)	[ʃuvis'kar]
pouring rain	**chuva** (f) **torrencial**	['ʃuva tohẽ'sjaw]
downpour	**aguaceiro** (m)	[agwa'sejru]
heavy (e.g., ~ rain)	**forte**	['fortʃi]
puddle	**poça** (f)	['posa]
to get wet (in rain)	**molhar-se** (vr)	[mo'ʎarsi]

fog (mist)	nevoeiro (m)	[nevo'ejru]
foggy	de nevoeiro	[de nevu'ejru]
snow	neve (f)	['nɛvi]
it's snowing	está nevando	[is'ta ne'vãdu]

86. Severe weather. Natural disasters

thunderstorm	trovoada (f)	[tro'vwada]
lightning (~ strike)	relâmpago (m)	[he'lãpagu]
to flash (vi)	relampejar (vi)	[helãpe'ʒar]

thunder	trovão (m)	[tro'vãw]
to thunder (vi)	trovejar (vi)	[trove'ʒar]
it's thundering	está trovejando	[is'ta trove'ʒãdu]

| hail | granizo (m) | [gra'nizu] |
| it's hailing | está caindo granizo | [is'ta ka'ĩdu gra'nizu] |

| to flood (vt) | inundar (vt) | [inũ'dar] |
| flood, inundation | inundação (f) | [ĩtrodu'sãw] |

earthquake	terremoto (m)	[tehe'mɔtu]
tremor, shoke	abalo, tremor (m)	[a'balu], [tre'mor]
epicenter	epicentro (m)	[epi'sẽtru]

| eruption | erupção (f) | [erup'sãw] |
| lava | lava (f) | ['lava] |

twister	tornado (m)	[tor'nadu]
tornado	tornado (m)	[tor'nadu]
typhoon	tufão (m)	[tu'fãw]

hurricane	furacão (m)	[fura'kãw]
storm	tempestade (f)	[tẽpes'tadʒi]
tsunami	tsunami (m)	[tsu'nami]

cyclone	ciclone (m)	[si'klɔni]
bad weather	mau tempo (m)	[maw 'tẽpu]
fire (accident)	incêndio (m)	[ĩ'sẽdʒju]
disaster	catástrofe (f)	[ka'tastrofi]
meteorite	meteorito (m)	[meteo'ritu]

avalanche	avalanche (f)	[ava'lãʃi]
snowslide	deslizamento (m) de neve	[dʒizliza'mẽtu de 'nɛvi]
blizzard	nevasca (f)	[ne'vaska]
snowstorm	tempestade (f) de neve	[tẽpes'tadʒi de 'nɛvi]

FAUNA

87. Mammals. Predators

predator	**predador** (m)	[preda'dor]
tiger	**tigre** (m)	['tʃigri]
lion	**leão** (m)	[le'ãw]
wolf	**lobo** (m)	['lobu]
fox	**raposa** (f)	[ha'pozu]
jaguar	**jaguar** (m)	[ʒa'gwar]
leopard	**leopardo** (m)	[ljo'pardu]
cheetah	**chita** (f)	['ʃita]
black panther	**pantera** (f)	[pã'tɛra]
puma	**puma** (m)	['puma]
snow leopard	**leopardo-das-neves** (m)	[ljo'pardu das 'nɛvis]
lynx	**lince** (m)	['lĩsi]
coyote	**coiote** (m)	[ko'jɔtʃi]
jackal	**chacal** (m)	[ʃa'kaw]
hyena	**hiena** (f)	['jena]

88. Wild animals

animal	**animal** (m)	[ani'maw]
beast (animal)	**besta** (f)	['besta]
squirrel	**esquilo** (m)	[is'kilu]
hedgehog	**ouriço** (m)	[o'risu]
hare	**lebre** (f)	['lɛbri]
rabbit	**coelho** (m)	[ko'eʎu]
badger	**texugo** (m)	[te'ʃugu]
raccoon	**guaxinim** (m)	[gwaʃi'nĩ]
hamster	**hamster** (m)	['amster]
marmot	**marmota** (f)	[mah'mɔta]
mole	**toupeira** (f)	[to'pejra]
mouse	**rato** (m)	['hatu]
rat	**ratazana** (f)	[hata'zana]
bat	**morcego** (m)	[mor'segu]
ermine	**arminho** (m)	[ar'miɲu]
sable	**zibelina** (f)	[zibe'lina]

marten	marta (f)	['mahta]
weasel	doninha (f)	[do'niɲa]
mink	visom (m)	[vi'zõ]

| beaver | castor (m) | [kas'tor] |
| otter | lontra (f) | ['lõtra] |

horse	cavalo (m)	[ka'valu]
moose	alce (m)	['awsi]
deer	veado (m)	['vjadu]
camel	camelo (m)	[ka'melu]

bison	bisão (m)	[bi'zãw]
wisent	auroque (m)	[aw'rɔki]
buffalo	búfalo (m)	['bufalu]

zebra	zebra (f)	['zebra]
antelope	antílope (m)	[ã'tʃilopi]
roe deer	corça (f)	['korsa]
fallow deer	gamo (m)	['gamu]
chamois	camurça (f)	[ka'mursa]
wild boar	javali (m)	[ʒava'li]

whale	baleia (f)	[ba'leja]
seal	foca (f)	['fɔka]
walrus	morsa (f)	['mɔhsa]
fur seal	urso-marinho (m)	['ursu ma'riɲu]
dolphin	golfinho (m)	[gow'fiɲu]

bear	urso (m)	['ursu]
polar bear	urso (m) polar	['ursu po'lar]
panda	panda (m)	['pãda]

monkey	macaco (m)	[ma'kaku]
chimpanzee	chimpanzé (m)	[ʃĩpã'zɛ]
orangutan	orangotango (m)	[orãgu'tãgu]
gorilla	gorila (m)	[go'rila]
macaque	macaco (m)	[ma'kaku]
gibbon	gibão (m)	[ʒi'bãw]

elephant	elefante (m)	[ele'fãtʃi]
rhinoceros	rinoceronte (m)	[hinose'rõtʃi]
giraffe	girafa (f)	[ʒi'rafa]
hippopotamus	hipopótamo (m)	[ipo'pɔtamu]

| kangaroo | canguru (m) | [kãgu'ru] |
| koala (bear) | coala (m) | ['kwala] |

mongoose	mangusto (m)	[mã'gustu]
chinchilla	chinchila (f)	[ʃĩ'ʃila]
skunk	cangambá (f)	[kã'gãba]
porcupine	porco-espinho (m)	['pɔrku is'piɲu]

89. Domestic animals

cat	**gata** (f)	['gata]
tomcat	**gato** (m) **macho**	['gatu 'maʃu]
dog	**cão** (m)	['kãw]
horse	**cavalo** (m)	[ka'valu]
stallion (male horse)	**garanhão** (m)	[gara'ɲãw]
mare	**égua** (f)	['ɛgwa]
cow	**vaca** (f)	['vaka]
bull	**touro** (m)	['toru]
ox	**boi** (m)	[boj]
sheep (ewe)	**ovelha** (f)	[o'veʎa]
ram	**carneiro** (m)	[kar'nejru]
goat	**cabra** (f)	['kabra]
billy goat, he-goat	**bode** (m)	['bɔdʒi]
donkey	**burro** (m)	['buhu]
mule	**mula** (f)	['mula]
pig, hog	**porco** (m)	['porku]
piglet	**leitão** (m)	[lej'tãw]
rabbit	**coelho** (m)	[ko'eʎu]
hen (chicken)	**galinha** (f)	[ga'liɲa]
rooster	**galo** (m)	['galu]
duck	**pata** (f)	['pata]
drake	**pato** (m)	['patu]
goose	**ganso** (m)	['gãsu]
tom turkey, gobbler	**peru** (m)	[pe'ru]
turkey (hen)	**perua** (f)	[pe'rua]
domestic animals	**animais** (m pl) **domésticos**	[ani'majs do'mɛstʃikus]
tame (e.g., ~ hamster)	**domesticado**	[domestʃi'kadu]
to tame (vt)	**domesticar** (vt)	[domestʃi'kar]
to breed (vt)	**criar** (vt)	[krjar]
farm	**fazenda** (f)	[fa'zẽda]
poultry	**aves** (f pl) **domésticas**	['avis do'mɛstʃikas]
cattle	**gado** (m)	['gadu]
herd (cattle)	**rebanho** (m), **manada** (f)	[he'baɲu], [ma'nada]
stable	**estábulo** (m)	[is'tabulu]
pigpen	**chiqueiro** (m)	[ʃi'kejru]
cowshed	**estábulo** (m)	[is'tabulu]
rabbit hutch	**coelheira** (f)	[kue'ʎejra]
hen house	**galinheiro** (m)	[gali'ɲejru]

90. Birds

bird	**pássaro** (m), **ave** (f)	['pasaru], ['avi]
pigeon	**pombo** (m)	['põbu]
sparrow	**pardal** (m)	[par'daw]
tit (great tit)	**chapim-real** (m)	[ʃa'pĩ-he'aw]
magpie	**pega-rabuda** (f)	['pega-ha'buda]
raven	**corvo** (m)	['korvu]
crow	**gralha-cinzenta** (f)	['graʎa sĩ'zẽta]
jackdaw	**gralha-de-nuca-cinzenta** (f)	['graʎa de 'nuka sĩ'zẽta]
rook	**gralha-calva** (f)	['graʎa 'kawvu]
duck	**pato** (m)	['patu]
goose	**ganso** (m)	['gãsu]
pheasant	**faisão** (m)	[faj'zãw]
eagle	**águia** (f)	['agja]
hawk	**açor** (m)	[a'sor]
falcon	**falcão** (m)	[faw'kãw]
vulture	**abutre** (m)	[a'butri]
condor (Andean ~)	**condor** (m)	[kõ'dor]
swan	**cisne** (m)	['sizni]
crane	**grou** (m)	[grow]
stork	**cegonha** (f)	[se'gɔɲa]
parrot	**papagaio** (m)	[papa'gaju]
hummingbird	**beija-flor** (m)	[bejʒa'flɔr]
peacock	**pavão** (m)	[pa'vãw]
ostrich	**avestruz** (m)	[aves'truz]
heron	**garça** (f)	['garsa]
flamingo	**flamingo** (m)	[fla'mĩgu]
pelican	**pelicano** (m)	[peli'kanu]
nightingale	**rouxinol** (m)	[hoʃi'nɔw]
swallow	**andorinha** (f)	[ãdo'riɲa]
thrush	**tordo-zornal** (m)	['tɔrdu-zor'nal]
song thrush	**tordo-músico** (m)	['tɔrdu-'muziku]
blackbird	**melro-preto** (m)	['mɛwhu 'pretu]
swift	**andorinhão** (m)	[ãdori'ɲãw]
lark	**laverca, cotovia** (f)	[la'verka], [kutu'via]
quail	**codorna** (f)	[ko'dɔrna]
woodpecker	**pica-pau** (m)	['pika 'paw]
cuckoo	**cuco** (m)	['kuku]
owl	**coruja** (f)	[ko'ruʒa]

eagle owl	bufo-real (m)	['bufu-he'aw]
wood grouse	tetraz-grande (m)	[tɛ'tras-'grãdʒi]
black grouse	tetraz-lira (m)	[tɛ'tras-'lira]
partridge	perdiz-cinzenta (f)	[per'dis sĩ'zẽta]

starling	estorninho (m)	[istor'niɲu]
canary	canário (m)	[ka'narju]
hazel grouse	galinha-do-mato (f)	[ga'liɲa du 'matu]
chaffinch	tentilhão (m)	[tẽtʃi'ʎãw]
bullfinch	dom-fafe (m)	[dõ'fafi]

seagull	gaivota (f)	[gaj'vɔta]
albatross	albatroz (m)	[alba'trɔs]
penguin	pinguim (m)	[pĩ'gwĩ]

91. Fish. Marine animals

bream	brema (f)	['brema]
carp	carpa (f)	['karpa]
perch	perca (f)	['pehka]
catfish	siluro (m)	[si'luru]
pike	lúcio (m)	['lusju]

| salmon | salmão (m) | [saw'mãw] |
| sturgeon | esturjão (m) | [istur'ʒãw] |

herring	arenque (m)	[a'rẽki]
Atlantic salmon	salmão (m) do Atlântico	[saw'mãw du at'lãtʃiku]
mackerel	cavala, sarda (f)	[ka'vala], ['sarda]
flatfish	solha (f), linguado (m)	['soʎa], [lĩ'gwadu]

zander, pike perch	lúcio perca (m)	['lusju 'perka]
cod	bacalhau (m)	[baka'ʎaw]
tuna	atum (m)	[a'tũ]
trout	truta (f)	['truta]

eel	enguia (f)	[ẽ'gia]
electric ray	raia (f) elétrica	['haja e'lɛtrika]
moray eel	moreia (f)	[mo'reja]
piranha	piranha (f)	[pi'raɲa]

shark	tubarão (m)	[tuba'rãw]
dolphin	golfinho (m)	[gow'fiɲu]
whale	baleia (f)	[ba'leja]

crab	caranguejo (m)	[karã'geʒu]
jellyfish	água-viva (f)	['agwa 'viva]
octopus	polvo (m)	['powvu]
starfish	estrela-do-mar (f)	[is'trela du 'mar]
sea urchin	ouriço-do-mar (m)	[o'risu du 'mar]

seahorse	cavalo-marinho (m)	[ka'valu ma'riɲu]
oyster	ostra (f)	['ostra]
shrimp	camarão (m)	[kama'rãw]
lobster	lagosta (f)	[la'gosta]
spiny lobster	lagosta (f)	[la'gosta]

92. Amphibians. Reptiles

snake	cobra (f)	['kɔbra]
venomous (snake)	venenoso	[vene'nozu]

viper	víbora (f)	['vibora]
cobra	naja (f)	['naʒa]
python	píton (m)	['pitɔn]
boa	jiboia (f)	[ʒi'bɔja]

grass snake	cobra-de-água (f)	[kɔbra de 'agwa]
rattle snake	cascavel (f)	[kaska'vɛw]
anaconda	anaconda, sucuri (f)	[ana'kõda], [sukuri]

lizard	lagarto (m)	[la'gartu]
iguana	iguana (f)	[i'gwana]
monitor lizard	varano (m)	[va'ranu]
salamander	salamandra (f)	[sala'mãdra]
chameleon	camaleão (m)	[kamale'ãu]
scorpion	escorpião (m)	[iskorpi'ãw]

turtle	tartaruga (f)	[tarta'ruga]
frog	rã (f)	[hã]
toad	sapo (m)	['sapu]
crocodile	crocodilo (m)	[kroko'dʒilu]

93. Insects

insect, bug	inseto (m)	[ĩ'sɛtu]
butterfly	borboleta (f)	[borbo'leta]
ant	formiga (f)	[for'miga]
fly	mosca (f)	['moska]
mosquito	mosquito (m)	[mos'kitu]
beetle	escaravelho (m)	[iskara'veʎu]

wasp	vespa (f)	['vespa]
bee	abelha (f)	[a'beʎa]
bumblebee	mamangaba (f)	[mamã'gaba]
gadfly (botfly)	moscardo (m)	[mos'kardu]

spider	aranha (f)	[a'raɲa]
spiderweb	teia (f) de aranha	['teja de a'raɲa]

dragonfly	**libélula** (f)	[li'bɛlula]
grasshopper	**gafanhoto** (m)	[gafa'ɲotu]
moth (night butterfly)	**traça** (f)	['trasa]

cockroach	**barata** (f)	[ba'rata]
tick	**carrapato** (m)	[kaha'patu]
flea	**pulga** (f)	['puwga]
midge	**borrachudo** (m)	[boha'ʃudu]

locust	**gafanhoto-migratório** (m)	[gafa'ɲotu-migra'tɔrju]
snail	**caracol** (m)	[kara'kɔw]
cricket	**grilo** (m)	['grilu]
lightning bug	**pirilampo, vaga-lume** (m)	[piri'lãpu], [vaga-'lumi]
ladybug	**joaninha** (f)	[ʒwa'niɲa]
cockchafer	**besouro** (m)	[be'zoru]

leech	**sanguessuga** (f)	[sãgi'suga]
caterpillar	**lagarta** (f)	[la'garta]
earthworm	**minhoca** (f)	[mi'ɲɔka]
larva	**larva** (f)	['larva]

FLORA

94. Trees

tree	árvore (f)	['arvori]
deciduous (adj)	decídua	[de'sidwa]
coniferous (adj)	conífera	[ko'nifera]
evergreen (adj)	perene	[pe'rɛni]
apple tree	macieira (f)	[ma'sjejra]
pear tree	pereira (f)	[pe'rejra]
sweet cherry tree	cerejeira (f)	[sere'ʒejra]
sour cherry tree	ginjeira (f)	[ʒĩ'ʒejra]
plum tree	ameixeira (f)	[amej'ʃejra]
birch	bétula (f)	['bɛtula]
oak	carvalho (m)	[kar'vaʎu]
linden tree	tília (f)	['tʃilja]
aspen	choupo-tremedor (m)	['ʃopu-treme'dor]
maple	bordo (m)	['bɔrdu]
spruce	espruce (m)	[is'pruse]
pine	pinheiro (m)	[pi'ɲejru]
larch	alerce, lariço (m)	[a'lɛrse], [la'risu]
fir tree	abeto (m)	[a'bɛtu]
cedar	cedro (m)	['sɛdru]
poplar	choupo, álamo (m)	['ʃopu], ['alamu]
rowan	tramazeira (f)	[trama'zejra]
willow	salgueiro (m)	[saw'gejru]
alder	amieiro (m)	[a'mjejru]
beech	faia (f)	['faja]
elm	ulmeiro, olmo (m)	[ul'mejru], ['ɔwmu]
ash (tree)	freixo (m)	['frejʃu]
chestnut	castanheiro (m)	[kasta'ɲejru]
magnolia	magnólia (f)	[mag'nɔlja]
palm tree	palmeira (f)	[paw'mejra]
cypress	cipreste (m)	[si'prɛstʃi]
mangrove	mangue (m)	['mãgi]
baobab	embondeiro, baobá (m)	[ẽbõ'dejru], [bao'ba]
eucalyptus	eucalipto (m)	[ewka'liptu]
sequoia	sequoia (f)	[se'kwɔja]

95. Shrubs

bush	**arbusto** (m)	[ar'bustu]
shrub	**arbusto** (m), **moita** (f)	[ar'bustu], ['mɔjta]
grapevine	**videira** (f)	[vi'dejra]
vineyard	**vinhedo** (m)	[vi'ɲedu]
raspberry bush	**framboeseira** (f)	[frãboe'zejra]
blackcurrant bush	**groselheira-negra** (f)	[groze'ʎejra 'negra]
redcurrant bush	**groselheira-vermelha** (f)	[grozɛ'ʎejra ver'meʎa]
gooseberry bush	**groselheira** (f) **espinhosa**	[groze'ʎejra ispi'ɲoza]
acacia	**acácia** (f)	[a'kasja]
barberry	**bérberis** (f)	['bɛrberis]
jasmine	**jasmim** (m)	[ʒaz'mĩ]
juniper	**junípero** (m)	[ʒu'niperu]
rosebush	**roseira** (f)	[ho'zejra]
dog rose	**roseira** (f) **brava**	[ho'zejra 'brava]

96. Fruits. Berries

fruit	**fruta** (f)	['fruta]
fruits	**frutas** (f pl)	['frutas]
apple	**maçã** (f)	[ma'sã]
pear	**pera** (f)	['pera]
plum	**ameixa** (f)	[a'mejʃa]
strawberry (garden ~)	**morango** (m)	[mo'rãgu]
sour cherry	**ginja** (f)	['ʒĩʒa]
sweet cherry	**cereja** (f)	[se'reʒa]
grape	**uva** (f)	['uva]
raspberry	**framboesa** (f)	[frãbo'eza]
blackcurrant	**groselha** (f) **negra**	[gro'zɛʎa 'negra]
redcurrant	**groselha** (f) **vermelha**	[[gro'zɛʎa ver'meʎa]
gooseberry	**groselha** (f) **espinhosa**	[gro'zɛʎa ispi'ɲoza]
cranberry	**oxicoco** (m)	[oksi'koku]
orange	**laranja** (f)	[la'rãʒa]
mandarin	**tangerina** (f)	[tãʒe'rina]
pineapple	**abacaxi** (m)	[abaka'ʃi]
banana	**banana** (f)	[ba'nana]
date	**tâmara** (f)	['tamara]
lemon	**limão** (m)	[li'mãw]
apricot	**damasco** (m)	[da'masku]
peach	**pêssego** (m)	['pesegu]

| kiwi | quiuí (m) | [ki'vi] |
| grapefruit | toranja (f) | [to'rãʒa] |

berry	baga (f)	['baga]
berries	bagas (f pl)	['bagas]
cowberry	arando (m) vermelho	[a'rãdu ver'meʎu]
wild strawberry	morango-silvestre (m)	[mo'rãgu siw'vɛstri]
bilberry	mirtilo (m)	[mih'tʃilu]

97. Flowers. Plants

| flower | flor (f) | [flɔr] |
| bouquet (of flowers) | buquê (m) de flores | [bu'ke de 'floris] |

rose (flower)	rosa (f)	['hɔza]
tulip	tulipa (f)	[tu'lipa]
carnation	cravo (m)	['kravu]
gladiolus	gladíolo (m)	[gla'dʒiolu]

cornflower	escovinha (f)	[isko'viɲa]
harebell	campainha (f)	[kampa'iɲa]
dandelion	dente-de-leão (m)	['dẽtʃi] de le'ãw]
camomile	camomila (f)	[kamo'mila]

aloe	aloé (m)	[alo'ɛ]
cactus	cacto (m)	['kaktu]
rubber plant, ficus	fícus (m)	['fikus]

lily	lírio (m)	['lirju]
geranium	gerânio (m)	[ʒe'ranju]
hyacinth	jacinto (m)	[ʒa'sĩtu]

mimosa	mimosa (f)	[mi'mɔza]
narcissus	narciso (m)	[nar'sizu]
nasturtium	capuchinha (f)	[kapu'ʃiɲa]

orchid	orquídea (f)	[or'kidʒja]
peony	peônia (f)	[pi'onia]
violet	violeta (f)	[vjo'leta]

pansy	amor-perfeito (m)	[a'mor per'fejtu]
forget-me-not	não-me-esqueças (m)	['nãw mi is'kesas]
daisy	margarida (f)	[marga'rida]

poppy	papoula (f)	[pa'pola]
hemp	cânhamo (m)	['kaɲamu]
mint	hortelã, menta (f)	[orte'lã], ['mẽta]

| lily of the valley | lírio-do-vale (m) | ['lirju du 'vali] |
| snowdrop | campânula-branca (f) | [kã'panula-'brãka] |

nettle	urtiga (f)	[ur'tʃiga]
sorrel	azedinha (f)	[aze'dʒinha]
water lily	nenúfar (m)	[ne'nufar]
fern	samambaia (f)	[samã'baja]
lichen	líquen (m)	['likē]

conservatory (greenhouse)	estufa (f)	[is'tufa]
lawn	gramado (m)	[gra'madu]
flowerbed	canteiro (m) de flores	[kã'tejru de 'floris]

plant	planta (f)	['plãta]
grass	grama (f)	['grama]
blade of grass	folha (f) de grama	['foʎa de 'grama]

leaf	folha (f)	['foʎa]
petal	pétala (f)	['pɛtala]
stem	talo (m)	['talu]
tuber	tubérculo (m)	[tu'berkulu]

| young plant (shoot) | broto, rebento (m) | ['brotu], [he'bētu] |
| thorn | espinho (m) | [is'piɲu] |

to blossom (vi)	florescer (vi)	[flore'ser]
to fade, to wither	murchar (vi)	[mur'ʃar]
smell (odor)	cheiro (m)	['ʃejru]
to cut (flowers)	cortar (vt)	[kor'tar]
to pick (a flower)	colher (vt)	[ko'ʎer]

98. Cereals, grains

grain	grão (m)	['grãw]
cereal crops	cereais (m pl)	[se'rjajs]
ear (of barley, etc.)	espiga (f)	[is'piga]

wheat	trigo (m)	['trigu]
rye	centeio (m)	[sē'teju]
oats	aveia (f)	[a'veja]

| millet | painço (m) | [pa'ĩsu] |
| barley | cevada (f) | [se'vada] |

corn	milho (m)	['miʎu]
rice	arroz (m)	[a'hoz]
buckwheat	trigo-sarraceno (m)	['trigu-saha'sēnu]

pea plant	ervilha (f)	[er'viʎa]
kidney bean	feijão (m) roxo	[fej'ʒãw 'hoʃu]
soy	soja (f)	['sɔʒa]
lentil	lentilha (f)	[lē'tʃiʎa]
beans (pulse crops)	feijão (m)	[fej'ʒãw]

COUNTRIES OF THE WORLD

99. Countries. Part 1

Afghanistan	**Afeganistão** (m)	[afeganis'tãw]
Albania	**Albânia** (f)	[aw'banja]
Argentina	**Argentina** (f)	[arʒẽ'tʃina]
Armenia	**Armênia** (f)	[ar'menja]
Australia	**Austrália** (f)	[aws'tralja]
Austria	**Áustria** (f)	['awstrja]
Azerbaijan	**Azerbaijão** (m)	[azerbaj'ʒãw]
The Bahamas	**Bahamas** (f pl)	[ba'amas]
Bangladesh	**Bangladesh** (m)	[bãgla'dɛs]
Belarus	**Belarus**	[bela'rus]
Belgium	**Bélgica** (f)	['bɛwʒika]
Bolivia	**Bolívia** (f)	[bo'livja]
Bosnia and Herzegovina	**Bósnia e Herzegovina** (f)	['bɔsnia i ɛrtsego'vina]
Brazil	**Brasil** (m)	[bra'ziw]
Bulgaria	**Bulgária** (f)	[buw'garja]
Cambodia	**Camboja** (f)	[kã'boja]
Canada	**Canadá** (m)	[kana'da]
Chile	**Chile** (m)	['ʃili]
China	**China** (f)	['ʃina]
Colombia	**Colômbia** (f)	[ko'lõbja]
Croatia	**Croácia** (f)	[kro'asja]
Cuba	**Cuba** (f)	['kuba]
Cyprus	**Chipre** (m)	['ʃipri]
Czech Republic	**República** (f) **Checa**	[he'publika 'ʃeka]
Denmark	**Dinamarca** (f)	[dʒina'marka]
Dominican Republic	**República** (f) **Dominicana**	[he'publika domini'kana]
Ecuador	**Equador** (m)	[ekwa'dor]
Egypt	**Egito** (m)	[e'ʒitu]
England	**Inglaterra** (f)	[ĩgla'tɛha]
Estonia	**Estônia** (f)	[is'tonja]
Finland	**Finlândia** (f)	[fĩ'lãdʒja]
France	**França** (f)	['frãsa]
French Polynesia	**Polinésia** (f) **Francesa**	[poli'nɛzja frã'seza]
Georgia	**Geórgia** (f)	['ʒɔrʒa]
Germany	**Alemanha** (f)	[ale'mãɲa]
Ghana	**Gana** (f)	['gana]
Great Britain	**Grã-Bretanha** (f)	[grã-bre'taɲa]
Greece	**Grécia** (f)	['grɛsja]

| Haiti | Haiti (m) | [aj'tʃi] |
| Hungary | Hungria (f) | [ũ'gria] |

100. Countries. Part 2

Iceland	Islândia (f)	[iz'lãʤa]
India	Índia (f)	['ĩʤa]
Indonesia	Indonésia (f)	[ĩdo'nɛzja]
Iran	Irã (m)	[i'rã]
Iraq	Iraque (m)	[i'raki]
Ireland	Irlanda (f)	[ir'lãda]
Israel	Israel (m)	[izha'ɛw]
Italy	Itália (f)	[i'talja]

Jamaica	Jamaica (f)	[ʒa'majka]
Japan	Japão (m)	[ʒa'pãw]
Jordan	Jordânia (f)	[ʒor'danja]
Kazakhstan	Cazaquistão (m)	[kazakis'tãw]
Kenya	Quênia (f)	['kenja]
Kirghizia	Quirguistão (m)	[kirgis'tãw]
Kuwait	Kuwait (m)	[ku'wejt]

Laos	Laos (m)	['laws]
Latvia	Letônia (f)	[le'tonja]
Lebanon	Líbano (m)	['libanu]
Libya	Líbia (f)	['libja]
Liechtenstein	Liechtenstein (m)	[liʃtẽs'tajn]
Lithuania	Lituânia (f)	[li'twanja]
Luxembourg	Luxemburgo (m)	[luʃẽ'burgu]

Macedonia (Republic of ~)	Macedônia (f)	[mase'donja]
Madagascar	Madagascar (m)	[mada'gaskar]
Malaysia	Malásia (f)	[ma'lazja]
Malta	Malta (f)	['mawta]
Mexico	México (m)	['mɛʃiku]
Moldova, Moldavia	Moldávia (f)	[mow'davja]

Monaco	Mônaco (m)	['monaku]
Mongolia	Mongólia (f)	[mõ'golja]
Montenegro	Montenegro (m)	[mõtʃi'negru]

| Morocco | Marrocos | [ma'hɔkus] |
| Myanmar | Birmânia (f) | [bir'manja] |

Namibia	Namíbia (f)	[na'mibja]
Nepal	Nepal (m)	[ne'paw]
Netherlands	Países Baixos (m pl)	[pa'jisis 'baɪʃus]
New Zealand	Nova Zelândia (f)	['nɔva zi'lãʤa]
North Korea	Coreia (f) do Norte	[ko'rɛja du 'nɔrtʃi]
Norway	Noruega (f)	[nor'wɛga]

101. Countries. Part 3

Pakistan	Paquistão (m)	[pakis'tãw]
Palestine	Palestina (f)	[pales'tʃina]
Panama	Panamá (m)	[pana'ma]
Paraguay	Paraguai (m)	[para'gwaj]
Peru	Peru (m)	[pe'ru]
Poland	Polônia (f)	[po'lonja]
Portugal	Portugal (m)	[portu'gaw]
Romania	Romênia (f)	[ho'menja]
Russia	Rússia (f)	['husja]
Saudi Arabia	Arábia (f) Saudita	[a'rabja saw'dʒita]
Scotland	Escócia (f)	[is'kɔsja]
Senegal	Senegal (m)	[sene'gaw]
Serbia	Sérvia (f)	['sɛhvia]
Slovakia	Eslováquia (f)	islɔ'vakja]
Slovenia	Eslovênia (f)	islɔ'venja]
South Africa	África (f) do Sul	['afrika du suw]
South Korea	Coreia (f) do Sul	[ko'rɛja du suw]
Spain	Espanha (f)	[is'paɲa]
Suriname	Suriname (m)	[suri'nami]
Sweden	Suécia (f)	['swɛsja]
Switzerland	Suíça (f)	['swisa]
Syria	Síria (f)	['sirja]
Taiwan	Taiwan (m)	[taj'wan]
Tajikistan	Tajiquistão (m)	[taʒiki'stãw]
Tanzania	Tanzânia (f)	[tã'zanja]
Tasmania	Tasmânia (f)	[taz'manja]
Thailand	Tailândia (f)	[taj'lãdʒja]
Tunisia	Tunísia (f)	[tu'nizja]
Turkey	Turquia (f)	[tur'kia]
Turkmenistan	Turquemenistão (m)	[turkemenis'tãw]
Ukraine	Ucrânia (f)	[u'kranja]
United Arab Emirates	Emirados Árabes Unidos	[emi'radus 'arabis u'nidus]
United States of America	Estados Unidos da América (m pl)	[i'stadus u'nidus da a'mɛrika]
Uruguay	Uruguai (m)	[uru'gwaj]
Uzbekistan	Uzbequistão (f)	[uzbekis'tãw]
Vatican	Vaticano (m)	[vatʃi'kanu]
Venezuela	Venezuela (f)	[vene'zwɛla]
Vietnam	Vietnã (m)	[vjet'nã]
Zanzibar	Zanzibar (m)	[zãzi'bar]

www.ingramcontent.com/pod-product-compliance
Lightning Source LLC
Chambersburg PA
CBHW071501070426
42452CB00041B/2064